# THE SCHOOL OF TOMORROW

# THE SCHOOL OF TOMORROW
## VALUES AND VISION

**Roger Crombie White**

**Open University Press**
Buckingham · Philadelphia

Open University Press
Celtic Court
22 Ballmoor
Buckingham
MK18 1XW

email: enquiries@openup.co.uk
world wide web: www.openup.co.uk
and
325 Chestnut Street
Philadelphia, PA 19106, USA

First Published 2000

A catalogue record of this book is available from the British Library

ISBN   0 335 20467 8 (pb)   0 335 20468 6 (hb)

*Library of Congress Cataloging-in-Publication Data*
White, Roger Crombie, 1949–
    The school of tomorrow : values and vision / Roger Crombie White.
      p.   cm.
    Includes bibliographical references and index.
    ISBN 0-335-20467-8 (pb) – ISBN 0-335-20468-6 (hb)
    1. Education, Secondary–Great Britain.   2. High schools–Great Britain.
  3. High school students–Great Britain–Interviews.   I. Title.
  LA635.W55 2000
  373.41–dc21
                                                                00–035613

Typeset by Graphicraft Limited, Hong Kong
Printed in Great Britain by St Edmundsbury Press Ltd,
Bury St Edmunds, Suffolk

To Joe, Caitlin and Malin

# Contents

# Preface

This is a book about education – specifically about issues to do with second-ary schooling.

The original plan was to explore the views of young people as to what kind of future they envisaged for the form and structure of education in the new millennium. Interviews were arranged with students aged between 14 and 18 who were attending independent and state-funded schools in Bristol, Liverpool, London, Oxfordshire, Staffordshire, North Ayrshire and York. Individually or within small groups they were encouraged to reflect on their educational experiences – the highs and the lows – and identify the things that had seemed most important in their years at school. Their comments provide an interesting snapshot of the current, lived experiences of adolescents in our secondary school system.

In considering possible changes and how differently things could be constructed in the future, the discussion led into an exploration of values – the rights and wrongs of particular courses of action, and the kinds of choices they would be making in their adult lives.

It was this issue of values that then became the centrepiece of the subsequent interviews with a number of adults involved with the world of education, including the Secretary of State for Education and Employment. Through their own responses they shared a great deal about their own values, and some of the choices they'd made as a consequence – how their own actions had been determined by particular sets of beliefs. In revealing their very human selves behind the official robes of office they offer very rich and personal insights into some of the issues that lie at the heart of any debate about education.

The comments by the British students and adults are juxtaposed with observations from Danish young people, as well as the Minister for

Education in Denmark, so as to offer a fascinating cross-cultural comparison of similarities and differences.

Put together, the dialogue between young people and adult educationalists that is reflected in the following pages offers an illuminating vision of the kind of educational system we might be able to create for the twenty-first century.

# Acknowledgements

There are many people I would like to thank for their help with this book.

The largest thank-you must go to the 77 students who gave time to be interviewed, who were very ready to enter into correspondence about their respective transcripts, and who were prepared to make their thoughts and ideas public: Keji Adedeji, Amel Alghrani, Jannine Antigha, Alistair Archibald, Lisa Ash, Oliver Banfield, Andrew Barber, Gillian Bayne, Alison Bentley, Katrine Bjerre, Laura Cook, Michael Court, Darron Cullen, Alex Deas, Jennifer Dew, Julia Ebdrup, Claire Evans, Lizzie Eves, Katy Garrett, Jaclyn Goddard, Jon Goode, Simon Goodhead, Ian Goodwin, Lilian Graversen, Leon Hendra, Kristian Henriksen, Tanya Heppell, Sarah Hewett, Catherine Hickey, Karen Holm, Clare Hudson, Mouna Ibrahim, Manmit Kaur, Josh Kay, Merete Kristensen, Victoria Laidlaw, Helene Lauridsen, Torsten Lauridsen, Richard Lewis, Karen Lloyd, Ann Karin Lodberg, Jody Lorimer, Ryan Lynch, David McGarry, Kirk Macrae, Paul Martin, Alex Mattin, Shafrin Nathoo, Rine Nielsen, Michael O'Callaghan, Lisa Osborne, Karim Palant, Mona Petersen, Katherine Poole, Jacob Rasmussen, Paula Reid, Katrine Rubjerg, Jendayi Selassie, Matthew Seymour, Amelia Smith, Judy Smith, Mark Smith, Nick Smith, Ole Sorensen, Peter Stidwell, Nawaz Sumar, Gareth Sutton, Asbjorn Thomasen, Lonni Vandborg, Carly Vaughan, Anne Vedel, Nicola Ward, Paul White, Deon Williams, Gary Williams, Nathalie Wirtz, Jonathan Wiseman. Good luck with whatever you go on to do.

In setting up these interviews, I am also very grateful to those staff in the schools and colleges in the different parts of the UK and in Denmark who showed considerable interest in this project and were so helpful in bringing together the various groups of students: Nils Andersen, Alan Easby, Phil Galbraith, Peter Gallie, Chrissie Garrett, Richard Gliddon, Marie Gray, Kaye Green, Knud Hagedorn, Anita Higham, Dorothy Holladay, Caroline

Inskip, Johanne Møller Sørensen, Dewi Phillips, Ray Priest, Allan Scott, Liz Teasdale, Julie Tridgell, Kathleen Zimac.

David Blunkett, Tim Brighouse, Anita Higham, Richard Pring, Nick Tate, Ted Wragg are all eminent in the world of education and I am very grateful that they were prepared to take the risk to air their views in a recorded interview, and allow these to be transcribed for wider dissemination. Their respective personal journeys illuminate the inspiration behind the vision and values that each of them holds. I am grateful to those in the DfEE, particularly John Connolly and Ralph Tabberer, who took the trouble to brief both me and the Secretary of State, so that the groundwork for that particular interview was well laid before we met.

To Margrethe Vestager, the Minister of Education for Denmark, and those in the Danish Ministry of Education (Thomas Lowell, Jens Marcussen, Bodil Andersen) who helped set up the interview and briefed the Minister accordingly, I am very grateful for the willingness to engage in debate and discussions about similarities and differences between the UK and Denmark.

Transcribing the tape recorded interviews was a daunting task, and I am indebted to the painstaking work of Elizabeth Rosengren who was in the middle of research for her own book at the same time, and to Vena Bunker, both of whom took great care with the accuracy of what went into print.

A collective thank-you to those colleagues at ASDAN and the University of the West of England, and to Keren Durant and Judith Stewart in particular, who have shown interest in this project and shared their own ideas and comments.

Discussions with Dave Brockington and Brian Fletcher in the context of our ASDAN work have helped develop my own thinking about 'social justice' – and have been much appreciated and enjoyed.

Shona Mullen at Open University Press deserves the credit for helping to mould the original idea for this book. The process of evolution of this book, by which ideas and chapters were revised and refined, illuminates the potential for creative interaction between publisher and author. My thanks to Shona for this.

Finally, to Christina Gray, who has commented on various versions of the manuscript and shared the journey, a very special thank-you. It is a better book as a result.

# The context

'I wish that there could be no wars and just peace, because when I see all those refugees on the television, I always think that if I was in that condition I would not like it at all. I hope that all the homeless people on the streets will become like us. We should all be the same.'

Jody Falla, age 9, in *Our World 2000* (Save the Children 1999)

An estimated two billion people watched the final of the World Cup in 1998, twice as many as those who tuned in to watch Prince Charles Windsor and Lady Diana Spencer get married in 1981. It is possible for significant world events to be experienced simultaneously by anything up to half the world's population. The dawn of the third millennium took place at different times around the world, but it was estimated that three billion people – half the world's population – were connected by satellite to watch revellers in Kiribati and New Zealand become the first people to enter the twenty-first century, or the countdown to midnight inside the Dome in Greenwich.

The power of technology to relay imagery and experience is so profound that we are often left reeling from the impact in our sitting rooms. In addition to rock concerts, celebrity weddings, coronations and international sporting events we can view wars, earthquakes, famine and poverty at the press of a button. Yet, strangely, at the same time, we are often bewildered as to what, if any, response we can make to these events. All the information in the world doesn't necessarily help us, assuming we even want to make a response.

Has this global highway brought us closer together as a species or further apart? Does the opportunity for enhanced communication at a personal level, through the telephone, fax and email, lead to heightened understandings and richer relationships? At a local level in our daily lives are we more or less sensitive to the needs of those around us? And where does it leave us in relation to our values and responsibilities?

In the UK we have been encouraged, through various 'charters', to take more notice of our rights. The patient's charter, the parent's charter and the traveller's charter have made it more explicit what standards we can expect from public services such as our hospitals, schools and transport, and what we can do if they fail to come up to standard. Competition between providers of these services has been promoted, in the belief that this would drive up the cost-effectiveness of such provision. We are all more conscious of our rights, and perhaps more clamorous for them. Yet at the same time we are aware of certain limitations – that these much-heralded rights don't necessarily translate into an improved quality of life.

Tabloid headlines alert us to the rationing that exists in a National Health Service that is having to confront an exponential increase in expectations of treatment against the backdrop of a finite budget. Fears are growing again about how we will manage as old age creeps up on us, because we know the workforce is shrinking in comparison to the number in retirement. As parents we can now choose where our children go to school, and the government provides a vast array of information in the form of school performance tables to help us with our choice. However, the reality for many parents is that choice is a chimera. Individual circumstances and experience can mean that the only realistic choice is the local school, which may have been abandoned by better resourced parents, with an eye to what seems like more impressive performance indicators from a neighbouring school. On the transport front we heard a lot about how rail privatization would lead to a better service, yet passengers now experience a growing number of delays and cancellations. In order to satisfy the performance indicators of punctuality, rail operators are simply extending journey times to increase the odds that trains will make it by the allotted hour.

In addition, we are preoccupied with crime and personal safety. Many people are reluctant to go out at night, or to venture into certain districts of our towns and cities. Parents are anxious for their children en route to school or the cinema. Alarm bells are sounding about the environment and the quality of our air, food and water. We are conscious some things are wrong, and we know our rights. But what of our responsibilities as individuals, either as residents in a particular street, or members of a local community, or inhabitants of particular towns or cities or rural areas, or citizens of a country, or the earth that we share with six billion others?

And to what extent are our responses as individuals influenced by the collective values of the culture in which we live, and how much do these collective values constrain or support us in making these responses? These are important questions. Consider, for instance, the following incidents, which could take place close to any corner shop in any street in any part of the United Kingdom.

A man comes out of the shop, slits open his packet of Regals, pushes a cigarette between his lips and tosses away the cellophane wrapper.

In the telephone box a group of 12-year-olds are giggling as one of their number tries to unscrew the coin box from its mountings.

Further up the street a middle-aged woman allows her poodle to defecate on the pavement, and hurries away from the offending pile.

In the house next to the corner shop the senior executive sighs with satisfaction in front of his computer screen as he sidesteps yet another tax claim.

The news-stand in front of the shop announces a 700 per cent bonus as part of the year's productivity payment for the boss of another privatized utility, which has generated massive profits for its shareholders.

Were we to observe any of these events, would we intervene in any way? And if we did, would the society of which we are part support us? Is there sufficient consensus about a core set of values that provides us with a solid point of reference for individual intervention? Or do we only do so when the event is something so starkly challenging and life-threatening that we are forced to respond, like witnessing a rape or a murder?

Much was written in the press at the time of Jamie Bulger's killing about the 'scores of people' who walked past the distressed little toddler as he was hauled on his way to a death at the hands of two 10-year-olds. There was a sense in which blame was being apportioned to these passive onlookers, without any acknowledgement that he could have been dragged past any one of us – and we would very likely have hesitated like they did, uncertain whether or not to intervene, immobilized by doubts about the seriousness of what we were witnessing, and our fear of repercussion from the youngsters, their friends, or their parents. Better not to get involved. What would we have done? And what would the people around us have done if we had acted?

These are uncomfortable questions, but they go to the heart of the sort of society we want to live in and the sort of education system that will mirror the values of such a society. We know enough about how groups function to know that it can be very difficult for individuals to take an initiative that they fear may be opposed by most members of the group – especially if that initiative will expose them to danger or ridicule. It is precisely why anti-discriminatory policies, enshrined in law, are so important as a backstop.

Let me illustrate this point with a more personal example.

Some years ago Christina and I were crossing London by underground, hurrying to catch a train from Paddington. It was close to rush hour. The train was full but not crowded, with only one or two people strap hanging. We were sitting in the middle of the carriage, near to the centre doors, idly doing what everyone else does on the underground: reading the adverts, checking Harry Beck's map above our heads, occasionally glancing at the people opposite, never long enough to make eye contact, but long enough to note the vast assortment of colours and shapes and accents and ages represented in this cross-section of humanity.

'Fucking nig nogs.'
Well, that's what it sounded like. I looked at Chris to see if she'd registered it too.

'Sodding little piccaninny children with smelly curry breath.'
The words seemed to come from the far end of the carriage. I leant sideways to see who was speaking. On one of the two pairs of facing seats beside the emergency door to the next carriage I could see an Asian couple sitting opposite their two children. The woman's face was wrapped in the shawl of her sari. The man stared impassively over the heads of his two little girls.

Perhaps it was all imagined? The carriage lurched as the train rounded a bend. Outside the heated compartment blue flashes lit up the snaking cables against the grime-black walls. I looked away and up at the map, noting it was only two stops to Paddington.

'Why don't you go home, you unwashed Pakki intruders? We don't want your sort round here. Scum round the edge of the Great British bath.'
It was impossible to ignore the voice. We looked along the carriage, past rows of expressionless eyes.

'Brown-bellied bastards. Go back to your mud huts and Tandoori titbits.'
The hatred in the voice was only matched by the vicious expression on the white boy's face. He was sitting on the edge of the parallel row of twin seats to the Asian family. Another youth sat beside him, facing two pink-haired, smiling girls. They all looked about 18 or 19.

'Do you hear what I'm saying, you lump of wombat shit?' The boy was looking straight at the father. 'Take your stinking family out of here.'
It was surely too absurd to be true? This must be some sort of theatrical event. Chris and I exchanged glances. No film crew in sight. We sat, uneasy, and uncertain, trying to make sense of the nonsense. The father was staring straight ahead, ignoring the torrent of abuse in his left ear. No-one else in the compartment uttered a sound. Only the rattle of the train and the flashing electric sparks outside the carriage held any semblance of reality. I noticed the woman's hand was squeezed against the arm of her husband, clutching the material of his finely cut jacket. This was no mock drama. It was horribly real – and unreal at the same time. Amidst the frozen inertia of the passengers the quiet dignity of the Asian family moved centre stage.

The clenched mouth was spewing its hostility inches from the brown ear, and still the man ignored it. What could I – we, anyone – do? What should we do? And would action simply make things worse?

The train began to slow down but the shouting continued. The carriage lurched to a halt, doors slid open, and the white vitriol dribbled into the dust on Edgware Road platform. No one moved or said anything. The silence stretched taut, as the seconds became minutes. Flickering eyes avoided each other, desperately looking for something to break the spell. Three policemen appeared with an elderly woman. The youth sat back, innocently smiling at his mates opposite.

'That's him, that's the one.' The elderly woman pointed with her umbrella.

'Right lad, come with us.' A restraining hand pressed down on the boy's shoulder.

'Take your fucking hands off me, copper,' the cockney voice snarled.

'Button your lip, son, just button it and come with me.' The boy stood up and was led onto the platform, his arm held by the man in blue.

'You'll need to come too,' one of the other policemen beckoned the Asian family off the train. It was then that the father spoke. 'It was him as well, and those two girls. It was horrible, spiteful, vicious.' He was shaking with angry reaction.

The other boy and the two young women were hustled onto the platform. The third policeman stood in the open doorway. 'Anyone else involved here sir?' The question was to the Asian man who shook his head.

'Right, that's it then, guard,' he nodded to the uniformed man beside him. 'You can move off now.'

The doors hissed shut; the train jolted and gathered speed. We caught a last glimpse of the father gesticulating to the listening policeman. Four sullen white faces stared back. The little girls were crying into their mother's sari. The black walls of the tunnel obscured the rest of the drama.

We spent the rest of the journey, and a long time afterwards, wondering what else we could and should have done and what others around us might have done had we acted.

That scene has often replayed in my mind. Although it is now nearly twenty years ago, I can still rekindle the tension of the train journey and frustration at my own inactivity, and the word cowardice bubbles up as well sometimes. There were choices being made in those moments of inactivity and I'd like to think that if it happened again I'd do something very different. That experience had powerful resonance for me a year later when I was travelling through Africa. Several times I found myself as the only white person in a crowd of black people, some of whom were very hostile. In Luanda, Angola, it was the day after the South African airforce had bombed the airport. In Bulawayo, Zimbabwe, it was nine months after independence and the public bus station was very definitely not a place for white people, unless you were mad or looking for trouble. At those moments it was hard to tell whether any of the faces in the crowd were friendly. I am better prepared for a rerun of the experience on the underground, and am clearer about the choices I would make and why I would make them – the values that would determine the action.

Values and choices are inextricably linked in the world of education. Take 'freedom of choice' and 'equality of opportunity' for instance. As a parent it is understandable if you want your child to do well at school. Because we have a system which allows 'parental choice' it is perfectly possible to shop around and consider schools beyond your immediate catchment area. If you have the financial resources, you can even buy your way into a particular school, believing that this may well enhance your child's chances of access to university. As an affluent and articulate parent you have some freedom of choice and are therefore susceptible to advertising and blandishments from schools that can use statistics to demonstrate an advantage.

However, as a local education authority or a government administration, you may feel you have a responsibility to ensure that the best possible provision exists for all children, and that parental wealth should not be a determinant of university entrance. You know that you have some excellent schools whose success is masked by unfair comparisons with schools that come from a different starting point. You believe the evidence that indicates that parental 'opting out' makes the improvement of state comprehensives more difficult. You want to do your best to ensure that opportunities are available on as equal a basis as possible, and you want to place some restrictions on parental choice of schools in order to ensure that every school has a reasonably comprehensive intake. You would like parents to have a sense of responsibility that extends beyond their individual child, and you hope they will make a choice that helps you to improve the schools in their catchment area; but you know you have limited capacity to influence the values that underpin that choice.

Interestingly, this particular issue is one about which many of the young people interviewed for this book express concerns that are echoed by many of the adults. The interplay of values and choices that have led them to support the comprehensive system of schooling is fascinating, and the way that they have arrived at some of these critical 'choice points' is illuminating, as you will read for yourself in subsequent chapters. I am grateful they were prepared to be so open about their personal journeys and the choices they made en route.

How often do you think back to your own choice points – those moments when you made a decision that very clearly shifted your life in a particular direction? Start with the moment of birth – not your choice of course, but an event in time that determined so much of what has followed for each of us.

When I start to think about this I realize that I could have been born anywhere in the world to any set of parents – at least to any mother. The mind wanders – a hut in an African village, a corrugated iron shack in a shanty town in Rio de Janeiro, a yurt on the central Asian steppes, a turf-roofed stone shelter in Greenland, a marble palace in India.

I felt the randomness of the chance of my own birth very strongly when I was hitch-hiking on my own from Zambia down to Gabarone in Botswana. I observed some dreadful consequences of poverty and malnourishment, and often wondered how I'd have coped had I emerged into consciousness on this planet as a boy or a girl in an enclave of mud huts two days' walk from the nearest road. I have played with the thought that I could have been born in one of a million places on my birthday. In many of these countries I would have had a 50:50 chance of surviving the first few years and would then have been working full-time by the age of 10.

Yet of the million possibilities, the reality turned out to be a hospital bed in Grantham to the wife of an RAF officer, and I grew up in a country where we'd never had it so good, where many of the diseases and illnesses that had wiped out huge percentages of previous generations had almost disappeared. Tuberculosis was no longer a killer; whooping cough and measles were serious but not usually life-threatening; even polio, whose very utterance held such dread for my parents' generation, was on the wane, although sometimes at school I'd meet children with legs in calipers. It could all have been very different, and the choices that would have flowed from the good or bad fortune of birth would have differed as a consequence.

However, the moment of birth is not a 'choice point'. It happens before we start creating our own luck – or not – and our own choice points. Can you identify those points in your life that have been momentous in terms of what you then went on to do?

One of mine was the first day I started teaching in a comprehensive school. I had left university, like many people of the 'sixties generation' unsure of what to do. In June 1970, we knew the statistics – that we represented an elite 6 per cent of the population – and we knew the world was our oyster. There was no doubt about getting a job; the only question was which one, and it didn't feel at all unusual to be one of many students who had finished university without a clear direction. I'd turned down offers from IBM and the RAF, having some vague idea about public service and the need to give 'something back' in return for the three very good years I'd enjoyed at university. I wasn't alone in that kind of thinking; it was part of the culture at the time.

So, in September 1970, after considerable prevarication during the summer holidays, I found myself walking through the gates of a Hampshire second-ary school at 8.30 one morning to take a post as a teacher of science and drama, having spent the previous day (and half the night) dithering on trains to and from where I'd been staying in London.

It was then, for the first time in my entire life, I met children who couldn't read and write.

Culture shock doesn't adequately describe what happened to me during that first day. By the time I staggered into bed and sank down into a deep, deep sleep, I had experienced a world that was completely alien to the high-flying chemistry graduate from the direct grammar school. It was a world where the written word carried no meaning for some of the 11-year-old children in my tutor group, and where IQ measurements seemed to indicate that four of them were on the cusp of being 'educationally subnormal'. I felt I had made a dreadful, dreadful mistake and it was only utter weari-ness that prevented me from taking the train back to London. And the next morning it was only a reluctance to let people down that kept me going through the day.

But within 48 hours I was hooked. The feelings of abject despair, which had threatened to overwhelm me when I appreciated my own inadequacies for the task of teaching, quickly evaporated. By the beginning of the second week I had felt touches of the euphoria that comes from a really good lesson. You will know what I mean – those moments when the interaction between you as a teacher and young people in the class is right on the cusp of their learning curve and you can see it soar upwards in an exponential arc. Exhilarating moments. And there were lots of them. I was totally, utterly, hopelessly hooked, and felt that, for the first time in my life, I had really found something I could give 100 per cent of myself to, without holding anything back.

In terms of jobs that decision to walk through those school gates was probably the most significant choice point in my entire working life.

Another was to move to Bristol in the mid-1970s to work with an emerging project for disaffected adolescents, which subsequently became the focus of a national dissemination project because of its remarkable success at motivating and reintegrating switched-off young people.

What drove these decisions? Why did I end up working with disadvantaged young people instead of working for a multinational company or continuing with flying training that might have led me into the pilot seat of a Harrier jet or Tornado bomber, and an opportunity to join the elite corps of pilots who saw 'active service' in the Falklands war, or some other war of the seventies and eighties? Or maybe I'd have been flying a desk or dead.

I can recall a brief conversation with my father in the mid-1970s. I had just resigned my position as head of chemistry at the comprehensive school in Hampshire to work with 'tail end' 14- and 15-year-old youngsters who had been 'trapped' in school because of the raising of the school-leaving age.

'You must be mad,' was his response to my news.

I started to explain that I felt they deserved something from formal education as well, that they had a right to something constructive, but I was conscious it all sounded rather weak and wishy-washy. The passion of belief in what had seemed like an important ideal on the steps of the Scotland Road Free School I'd visited some months before was hard to sustain in the coffee bar one street away from the Ministry of Defence building in the heart of central London.

'I suppose I just feel that the system's not fair,' I ended rather lamely.

'But you're not going to change anything. It's pretty pointless trying to help these sorts of characters. There are always going to be people at the bottom of the heap. There's no career in this sort of work, boy.'

I wish now I'd been able to offer him the story about the dying starfish that Ted Wragg so eloquently recounts on page 134.

I wish, too, I'd been able to explain to him where this sense that some things weren't 'fair' came from. I felt it very strongly then, and I feel it very strongly still. But I can't tell you where it originated, or why. Maybe it was an aggregation of events and experiences that, despite my rather conservative upbringing, led me to a point where notions of a 'just society' came to feel significant. Perhaps, as Tim Brighouse says much more eloquently on page 99, it's close to religion.

I just know that when I watched the Tory party being counted out in the early morning of 2 May 1997 I felt a mixture of relief and elation. This is not really a party political point. There seemed to be an overwhelming reaction from the majority of the electorate towards the arrogance, the meanness, and the 'me first' set of values that came to characterize that particular administration of the eighties and nineties, which culminated in a series of high-profile scandals. The shift towards a more equitable distribution of wealth, which had been taking place under previous administrations (both Conservative and Labour) in the sixties and seventies, was effectively reversed by the Thatcher/Major brand of conservatism. It was an administration for whom a belief in 'social justice' seemed to be very low on the agenda and Labour, Liberal Democrat and many Conservative voters had had enough (O'Farrell 1999).

It was replaced by an administration that claimed a rather different set of core values, and had set out one plank of its market stall as 'Education, Education, Education', with a clear commitment to the state-funded sector. I felt that we might see the ascendancy of a set of values that put 'equality of opportunity' and 'social justice' high on the reforming agenda. I was optimistic about the wind of change that would blow through our education system, although I was realistic enough to know that there are huge obstacles within our system and our pervading culture.

I am optimistic because I have seen and experienced, not so very far from our own shores, a country where such values actually operate as a determinant of educational provision and social welfare. Those of you who have spent any time in Scandinavia will know what I mean. Danish schools, for instance, emphasize the importance of the affective domain, both through their structures and their curriculum. This is not to say that they disregard the cognitive, but they see the former as needing nurturing as a precursor for the latter. Pre-school provision is organized around cooperative play and practical activity. Reading and writing are not specifically encouraged in the early years, and formal teaching begins at age 7. There is a widespread belief among school teachers and pupils that 'being better' than other pupils at school work doesn't mean you're a 'better' person. There is no national testing before 16 and no attempt to produce league tables for school performance. Access to further and higher education is not a privilege for the few whose chances can be maximized by attendance at a number of selective schools. Ninety-three per cent of young people continue with education and training after the age of 16, and all of it is free, paid for by a high level of taxation that the majority of the voting population are consistently prepared to support (Hastrup 1995; Ministry of Education in Denmark 1998a).

Chapters 14 and 15 consider some aspects of Scandinavian education in more detail, and draw on interviews with Danish sixth form students and Margrethe Vestager, the Minister of Education for Denmark, to illustrate certain points of comparison. At this stage it is just worth noting that some of the core values so evident throughout their education system find echoes in many of the values espoused by the other contributors to this book. If enough people assert them and we have an administration that promotes them, we may just have an opportunity in these opening years of the twenty-first century to create a rather different educational system to the one that has dominated our country and our culture for the past two hundred years.

The comments in this book may help to bring that vision closer to reality.

# 2

# Young people's comments about school

'How about if at school everyone had their own massaging chair. So whenever you felt worn out, you pressed a button and you got a free massage!'
Danielle Holmes, age 8, in *Our World 2000* (Save the Children 1999)

The young people interviewed for this chapter came from schools in various parts of the UK. The criteria for selection was simply that they were in their last year of compulsory schooling (S4 in Scotland and Year 11 in England), were intending to continue with some sort of education and training beyond 16, and were interested to talk about a whole range of issues to do with their school experience. In some cases these were one-to-one interviews, in other cases small groups. Generally, it worked better with groups where the 'critical mass' was large enough for the interplay of energies to act as a catalyst for discussion.

I had a prepared checklist of questions, but the interviews very quickly developed a life of their own as the young people brought up issues they really wanted to talk about, and I encouraged them to do this. They knew that they were contributing to a book that was looking to the future in relation to how schools and the process of teaching and learning might be rather different. They also knew that their comments might be used as the basis for some questions to adults in positions of authority and influence. I encouraged them to look forwards; inevitably some of them glanced backwards as a point of reference and many of their comments reflected their current concerns and preoccupations.

Subsequently, the transcript of the interview was sent to each person involved, and I encouraged them to edit and extend their comments and return them. Most of them took this opportunity and I selected extracts from the returned transcripts to build up a picture that was a fair representation of the spread of opinion and observation. This edited compilation was returned to them again, for final approval. Put together, they provide some illuminating insights into the contemporary experience of secondary pupils.

## On the transfer from primary to secondary school . . .

'It can be difficult when you first come up to secondary school because you hear lots of rumours about what they are going to do to you. You lose all your friends. I was put in a class with only one person from my school and I didn't know him that well, so I had to make new friends.'

(Richard)

'It's a completely new experience and schools can be very cruel places. I don't think people who haven't got friends are really helped by other people. They're just overlooked.'

(Paula)

'Some people find it hard to make friends and there may be no-one who likes them really. It was easier for me because I had an older brother in the school which helped, but you soon start to get your own friends. I think the hardest thing is not trying too hard to look for friends. You've got to be yourself because it won't work out if you try to be someone else just to make friends.'

(Oliver)

'My primary school was tiny, with about 70 pupils. Coming to a school like this seemed so massive. It was really quite frightening. It took me a week just to find my way round.'

(Claire)

'I didn't look forward to going. At the one I went to all the lads who went there were supposed to be bullies, and me and my mates were really worried about going. It seemed massive compared to junior school. A thousand pupils compared to the two hundred at primary school. I felt lonely. But it was better than I thought it was going to be.'

(Robert)

'The really difficult bit was having to talk to so many people I didn't know. The older kids looked so massive and they'd be coming up and asking you questions, and you'd want to run the other way.'

(Ryan)

'The thing is that when you come up to secondary school you would only come up with three or four people that you know from primary school, but now I can speak to most of the people in my year and the years below and above me.'

(Darron)

'There's a tremendous distance between you and the teachers. There are so many more people and life seems much more complex.'

(Brian)

'It really hit me coming from junior school where I'd had women teachers all the time, to a school where I had lots of male teachers. I was really worried.'

(Jayne)

'You're at the top in primary school, and then you start at the bottom in secondary school and have to go all the way up again.'

(Catherine)

'It feels weird being at the beginning again, especially if not a lot of people that you know are going to your secondary school. Here they made an effort to put all your friends in the same tutor group, so that you wouldn't feel out of place.'

(Shafrin)

## On advice to primary pupils . . .

'If I was talking to a pupil about to start secondary school, I'd say don't worry about what you've heard from other people, because it's not true.'

(Alistair)

'Try and make friends straight away, because no-one else will have a lot of friends either. Just go over and talk to other people and meet them. As soon as you've got your friends, you'll feel a lot more com-fortable! You can't push yourself, but don't be stand offish either.'

(Oliver)

'You've got to try and make the effort, because you know if you don't that you won't get anywhere.'

(Claire)

'It's scary for the first week, but when you get to know people and you get to know teachers it's great, because you find a whole new circle of friends, so you'll have your friends at home as well as at school.'

(Brian)

'It's great fun; there's loads of different things to do, and you can enjoy being more grown up. Your parents start to treat you differently as well. Whereas in junior school they're always there for every concert and to pick you up after school, at secondary school you start to manage on your own.'

(Gillian)

'I'd say, "Get involved and listen." If you are forced to sit in a class you might as well listen because then you don't have to do as much homework.'

(Robert)

'You've got to be strong to get through it. It will be quite tough. School is like anywhere where there's a lot of people and you are just a small per cent of the group. You've got to be confident.'

(Carly)

'You've got to think it. In Year 6 I used to be very quiet and shy but I used to make myself think I was strong. And it looked like that to everyone else. So in the end I felt I was strong from just thinking I was.'

(Mouna)

'I remember my big brother telling me that I was going to get my head flushed down the toilet on my birthday. I'm going to make my little brother worry about it too, just to tease him!'

(Deon)

'I'd say it's going to be easier if you've got friends from primary school coming up with you, because then you've got a group already – you don't have to start afresh making brand new friends. But you make friends anyway, when you're here.'

(Jendayi)

## On friendship . . .

'I think it makes a big difference when your friends are in lessons with you, because you're more confident when you're with them. You enjoy coming to school and even if you're talking a lot, you work better because of the pleasant atmosphere.'

(Amelia)

'One of the interesting things about holidays is that you hate school, but by the time you come back, you're looking forward to it again. During the holidays you get bored because your friends are living on the other side of town or out of town and you don't see them. School is a good place to socialize.'

(Darron)

'Friends is the most important part of going to school. If you haven't got a good friend, then you're not going to enjoy school very much.'

(Paul)

'There's only one person I know of who hasn't got friends. But he's quite clever and that makes it OK because he can just sit there and do millions of work and he doesn't have to talk to anyone at all.'

(Sarah)

'What's good is being around your friends and having lots of activities that are arranged, such as school trips.'

(Richard)

'I've never walked up to anyone and said, "Oh, will you be my friend?" The best way of making friends is playing a football match or something like that. Everybody on the pitch is your friend.'

(Deon)

'Maybe in PE lessons when we have to get in teams then you get talking to someone. That's how I made friends. Or, "Do you want me to paint your nails?" Or in lessons there might be a spare seat and you might just sit there and start talking.'

(Jendayi)

## On curriculum issues . . .

'I like experiments and research in science. I enjoy maths. I can't do it as well as the others, but I like it. And I've always liked art from the first time I could hold a pen. I love drawing.'

(Mouna)

'This school is really good for music and all the arts really. It offers GCSE drama now as well.'

(Catherine)

'It's a good school. If you're good at something, then they bring it out in you. If you're not so good at something, then they try and get you better at it.'

(Carly)

'Doing the Youth Award Scheme has been brilliant because of all the opportunities it gives you to do things outside of school as well as in school and have them counted for your certificate. Going to the leisure centre, or making music, or doing a community project, which are all fun to do, can be included for your award. It really helps with your confidence as well, because you find yourself having a go at things that you didn't think you could do.'

(Ryan)

'Some of the subject stuff you learn in school, like formulae in maths or dates in history, you're not really going to need that in the real world, but the thing you do need to know is how to learn, because later on when you get a job and there are skills to be learnt, you'll be able to pick them up quicker.'

(Robert)

'I enjoy learning new things: something different every day. It's good because it's more interesting.'

(Paula)

## On other benefits of being in school . . .

'Meeting new people and learning how to get on with them is important. And there's much more sport of course in secondary school.'

(Oliver)

'Having to talk to new people was the hardest thing about being in secondary school. I used to feel really nervous. But now, even though I'm still nervous, like doing this interview with you, I know I can do it and put my views across. This school has given me so much confidence. I've enjoyed coming here, although I'd like to see more opportunities for girls to play football and more time for music.'

(Gillian)

'You've got to have schools because otherwise you'll be thick. If you haven't got any education, you won't get very far in life.'

(Alistair)

'It helps your confidence because you get used to talking in front of thirty other people, so that when you go out to work and you have to present a project for a company, you'll have been used to doing it.'

(Audrey)

'It helps you prepare for life. Obviously you're going to meet people in life that you don't get on with, and you've just got to learn to deal with that. You're going to meet people that are different to you, different culturally, different religion. That's good because it helps you.'

(Catherine)

## On what makes for good teaching . . .

'Allowing a bit of conversation between you when you work, with a few jokes to help lighten the atmosphere.'

(Richard)

'Any teacher can be interesting, however old they are. It's the way they do it that's important. If they are pushing you all the time and never leave you alone, like some teachers go on and on about the neatness of your work, then that just doesn't encourage you at all.'

(Oliver)

'When a good teacher inspires and makes you want to learn, as opposed to feeling that you have to learn all these facts that, after GCSEs, you will have forgotten. It's someone who teaches from the knowledge in their head and their own experiences, not simply from a textbook, because we could be doing that ourselves.'

(Amelia)

'If you like the teacher you want to work well for them to get good grades. Good teachers learn to know how fast you can work and then they push to your maximum, without trying to make everyone work at the same pace.'

(Paula)

'When you have a teacher that you like it can be fun. I had a teacher of history who didn't get angry if we asked him personal questions, like where he was going for his holidays. He wouldn't tell us obviously, but he'd say, "Oh, I'm going to Mars and I've got my spaceship ready." He was a really nice teacher.'

(Mouna)

'If a teacher says, "You can get an A" and is pushing me to get an A, I will work for that A. But if the teacher says, "Oh, I'm not sure about you. You could do better, but I think you're going to stay on a D", then I'll give up.'

(Carly)

'One of my best teachers explains everything and if people don't get it the first time, then he just says it again and doesn't mind doing that. It's very different to those teachers who, when you ask them to explain something again they say you haven't been listening, even when it's just that you don't understand.'

(Lisa)

'Someone who gets the point across, without being so strict that you can't have a social talk. Somebody who hasn't forgotten the meaning of childhood and that our school years are undoubtedly the most important ones of our life.'

(Darron)

'They should be interested in what you're doing, but I don't think I'd talk about very personal things with a teacher. They can't really appreciate your situation.'

(Audrey)

'We need conversation, not just a one-way telling off. If you feel like you're getting a bit more respect, then you're going to respect them, so you're going to work for them.'

(Richard)

'There's one teacher who always treats us like first years. "Stand up, tuck your shirts in", and we have to wait around till everyone's quiet and we have to be facing the front. If we don't then we have to stand up again and do the whole thing again. Every lesson. We could have more responsibility now that we're in Year 11. Quite often we're still treated like infants.'

(Claire)

'The younger teachers are more laid back. It's like they can remember what it's like to be at school, so they understand you better.'

(Alastair)

'The good teachers are the ones who know how to listen as well as talk, who don't make you feel that your opinion isn't worth anything. It's not age that's important; it's their attitude to young people. There are some who don't seem to enjoy what they're doing, and there are others who seem so enthusiastic about their subjects. It's brilliant being with those sort of teachers.'

(Gillian)

'Teachers are baby-sitters really. They look after us whilst our parents go out to work.'

(Paul)

'A good teacher is someone with a lot of patience, who tries to show no favouritism at all, and who is prepared to listen to your point of view. When you reach our age, you develop your own opinions. If teachers were to hold more discussions in the classroom, the teacher–pupil relationship could improve a great deal.'

(Sarah)

'Good teachers are those who help pupils, especially those who are finding things really difficult, without making them feel stupid because they don't understand something. I've got some really good teachers and you don't worry about asking them questions. They never say, "I've told you that ten minutes ago, were you daydreaming?", even if you probably were!'

(Ryan)

'If a teacher is shouting at you, you are not likely to do a lot of work, because you're going to be upset all through that lesson, annoyed at the teacher. Just to spite the teacher you won't do any work.'

(Shafrin)

'You've got to understand teenagers, and be able to have a laugh with children as well as making sure you get all the work done. It's the way they talk to you that's important. They might just tell you what to do and leave you to get on with it. But some people might not understand what to do, so they need to explain it fully, step by step.'

(Jendayi)

## On multicultural issues . . .

'The school does special events and posters when it's a particular holiday: they have Asian days, African days, all these different things. The Head is very strong on racism. He'll spend a whole day making sure it's all sorted out. He'll go round the classes and talk to all the groups and explain the situation if it's a big deal. Otherwise he'll talk to the person and bring their parents in to sort it out if necessary.'

(Mouna)

'You learn about other religions and other backgrounds. It prepares you for when you're older. You might travel abroad.'

(Catherine)

'This school prepares you really well for living in a multicultural world. It's not like this is a whole white country or a whole black country, or a whole Asian country. It's all mixed together. You're going to meet them all the time, so you might as well get used to it and not be racist. I'm not being funny, but it's older people who are more racist than the younger ones.'

(Carly)

'You get a chance to meet different types of people here and you come into contact with different cultures and races. Racism is emotional though. It's hard to tackle.'

(Shafrin)

'I'd rather be in an environment where there's white people, black people, Asian people; all sorts. In my friendship groups it's all mixed.'

(Jendayi)

'There's less racism here because it's a multicultural school.'

(Deon)

'In my previous school a lot of the students were racist. They admitted
it and they showed off, so I had to go through it. The school line was,
"You're different and we accept it, but we can't do any more for you.
All the rest is personal, so it's nothing to do with the school." You're
different was pushed in our faces all the time. They said about the
kids, "Oh, they won't do it again, so don't worry about it, we'll help
you through." It made you feel different, like the other kids weren't
doing anything wrong. They never made it a big thing, but it was a
very big thing.'

(Anon.)

## On bullying . . .

'I'd really like to get rid of this in our school. It can be people making
sly comments in the classroom, or having a go at you for doing your
homework better than anyone else. I think it's something to do with
the person not having something, or something happened to them in
their childhood. You don't walk up to a person and start having a fight
with them for no reason. It's got to be something inside you that
makes you do it. Perhaps something's happened, like your mum's died,
and you want to take it out on another kid who seems to have everything in the class.'

(Claire)

'I reckon it fades out in the sixth form, because I think it's the people
who are not so bright that they have to pick on others just to make
themselves look big. Most of those people leave at 16.'

(Richard)

'The trouble is that if the bully is more popular than the person being
picked on, then people will just ignore it. No-one is going to stand up
to the most popular person. It's not about being tough, because there's
a very big difference between people that can stand up for themselves
and people that are bullies. Bullies go looking for trouble, picking on
people that aren't able to defend themselves. Being able to stand up for
yourself is something that you know you can do and other people
know you can do it if it comes to the crunch. Bullying is not always
physical though.'

(Paula)

'The worst thing is when people are two-faced to you. Like one day
they'll be really friendly when they're together with you alone, but when
they're in a group they work it so that everyone hates you. That's the
worst kind because you don't know whether to trust them or not.'

(Alistair)

'I think schools should be tougher on the big kids who set on little kids like me. You get fed up being picked on, so you stay away from school, which makes it worse. But it's not really your fault – it's the fault of the people making you stay away.'

(Robert)

'Having friends is really important, so that you can stand up for each other when you need some help.'

(Ryan)

'There's a bit of bullying lower down the school, but by the time you get to Year 10, everyone knows each other so well. There are still arguments between friends though.'

(Carly)

'I was at the bus stop once and a girl was being bullied by someone who used to pick on my sister. He was shouting at her and calling her all sorts of names. I just went mad at him, and he's never done it again.'

(Catherine)

'This school has its fair share of fights, but not bullying type of fights. Just "one-off" fights and that's it.'

(Deon)

## On ability groupings . . .

'In Year 7 and Year 8 I was in with my friends, but they weren't as bright as me, so they were put into different gradings when we moved into Year 9. When I was with them it was good, because I could help them and I learned more by helping them. But in Year 9 when I was put in a class with people I didn't know, I felt stupid asking them for help. That's where it went wrong for me. I would have preferred to stay with my friends and I'd have worked much better being able to talk with them. I think splitting friends up is un-necessary, especially using A, B and C grades. People in C grades must feel really stupid compared to their friends who've been put into A grades.'

(Jayne)

'My best mate was put into the bottom group, so I hardly saw him once we were split up. It was hard for both of us, because he decided he must be really thick and he kept taking the piss out of me for being a keener. We didn't stay good friends for very long.'

(Robert)

'If groups are mixed ability it can go too slowly for some people, or go too fast for others.'

(Mouna)

'I think it's helpful to put people in different classes, because then you have a place for the people that understand more and another for the people that understand less.'

(Shafrin)

'It's better to be in a working environment where everyone's on the same level, than with some people struggling, so you've got to wait for them to catch up. If people are rushing ahead it makes you feel bad because they're watching you and you're thinking I'm behind. In maths I'm in the intermediate group which is fine. If I was in a higher group I'd be pressured and I wouldn't be able to handle that. If I was in foundation I wouldn't be able to get the grades I wanted to do A levels. So the one I'm in is OK.'

(Jendayi)

## On disruptive behaviour . . .

'There's a lot of kids in classes who go round and disrupt classrooms, and I think that's bad. We're here to learn, and to mess around just seems to be a complete waste of time to me. I don't want to be in school any longer than I need to, but I've got to do it to get my GCSEs and my A levels and I don't want my learning disrupted.'

(Claire)

'More teachers' time is spent on those who don't want to learn than is spent on those that have difficulties learning but want to learn. I don't think as much time should be spent on the troublemakers.'

(Lisa)

'Kids who lark around are wasting time. When they leave school they're going to say to themselves, "I knew I should have done that", and they'll look back and see they've made a big mistake.'

(Paul)

'There's got to be a line and after that it's serious. There's one teacher who says, "Right, you'll be out if you do that again", and then there's this kid who keeps giving her verbal abuse, and she doesn't do anything. She says, "Shaun! Out." And he says, "No I'm not going", and she just says, "Be quiet then." All her threats are false.'

(Richard)

'Knowing where the line is and everything, and if we go over that line then we are in trouble. Teachers need to be firm; it's no good if they give out threats and don't take any action. In the first lessons you really push to find out where the line is between having a laugh and getting told off. If you don't find a line then you're just going to keep going and so is everyone else when they don't see anything happening.'

(Paula)

'I remember in our first science lesson we just mucked about and the teacher never told us off. Well, he'd tell us off but we'd just keep doing it and he'd never carry out any threats and everyone would laugh at him in the class. It was hopeless.'

(Brian)

## On the state of the buildings . . .

'Every school has its bad points. The bad one in ours was the buildings.'

(Audrey)

'I think a school has got to look good. If it doesn't look good, then people won't be attracted to it, and aren't going to treat it with much respect. We need to spend more money on text books, equipment, and more teachers, instead of crazy projects like the Millennium Dome.'

(Claire)

'It's like the toilets which need to be sorted. If you could make them good, then people would respect them and won't do anything to harm them.'

(Paula)

'Except that there are some people who don't like nice respectable places that would just go and trash them!'

(Jayne)

'We need lockers, but we're told that there's not enough room in the school and they cost too much money. Yet you need somewhere that's your own to keep things safe, or you spend the whole day carrying everything around on your back, like a snail.'

(Brian)

'It must be hard to keep it looking good when so many children are in and out of it all day – particularly when it's wet and blowing a gale. It makes a difference to how you feel about it though, when you can see that somebody cares about a place. They're really trying to sort out environmental things here, with recycling projects and such like. The seagulls help because they clear up some of the litter at the end of lunch breaks!'

(Gillian)

## On school uniform . . .

'I think it helps parents to have a school uniform, because they don't have to buy ten pairs of trousers and a million shirts. If we didn't have a school uniform, then there would be people walking around in their Adidas shoes and Reebok jumpers to look big or cool or hard, and others who just couldn't afford the latest gear.'

(Claire)

'I think it's to do with power. The teachers like you all to look the same. There's a big thing here about having your shirt tucked in. If you're walking round at lunchtime with your shirt hanging out, teachers will come round and say, "Tuck your shirt in." I think you should be able to wear what you want within reason. If anything, it'll make you work better because you're more comfortable. If I went to college it'd be my choice and I could wear what I like. It makes you more responsible.'

(Oliver)

'I think trainers should be allowed. But I appreciate it might cause arguments between kids who'd not got them, or who'd got the wrong sort and then have the mick taken out of them.'

(Paul)

'I think we should have trainers because our school shoes get wrecked walking to school. I have to come two and a half miles to school, so it'd be more sensible to do it in trainers. They're meant for training!'

(Sarah)

'Wearing uniform helps to eliminate prejudice and discrimination towards poorer students, as it becomes very hard to distinguish how "scruffy" or "trendy" a person is from their uniform.'

(Darron)

'If I didn't have a uniform, I'd wake up in the morning and think, "Oh my God, what am I going to wear?" There are two sides to this because I don't particularly like the uniform, but I'd get a bit stressed about what to wear if we didn't have one.'

(Lisa)

'You see people who come in on non-uniform days who are wearing last year's clothes or tight leggings or whatever and they have the mick taken out of them. For a day it's all right, but if that happened to that person every day it would be bad. So I think uniform's a good thing.'

(Robert)

'If we didn't have a uniform then people would moan if they went into art and got paint on their clothes and it wouldn't come off.'

(Amelia)

'You get no class distinction with uniform. It doesn't matter whether your parents have a good wage or have financial problems: you all wear the same. And if your parents aren't working, you're given a grant.'

(Brian)

## On private schooling ...

'I went to a private school for a couple of years. A lot of the people there were well off. When I started I had this really wild accent, and they used to make fun of me. In assembly when the word Lord came up in prayers they all used to go, "Lorrrrrrd!", like that. I've got a local accent, but that's just me, that's who I am. Just because I've got an accent doesn't mean I'm any less clever than someone who goes to private school. They're different. I wouldn't say they're necessarily better. If you want the education you've got to do it yourself.'

(Catherine)

'The education you get from a private school is good which is why people pay for their children to go to private schools. It doesn't necessarily mean that they're going to get better results, but parents don't want their children to mix with the wrong people though.'

(Mouna)

'If a kid wants to get their education, then they're going to get it wherever they go. What matters is self-motivation.'

(Carly)

'My mum says you will get better results if you go to a private girls' school. I think I probably would have got better results – maybe.'

(Jendayi)

'There must be some children being sent to private school that come out with rubbish grades. I think it's all in the mind if you're going to get good grades or not. There's people in this school who have been through it without going to private schools and they've come out with 11 A stars.'

(Deon)

## On concerns beyond the school walls . . .

'Have you seen how many houses are boarded up with nobody living in them and yet when they get taken over by squatters, who aren't necessarily doing any harm, they are hauled out and made to live on the streets again? If they're looking after the place, why shouldn't they have a roof over their heads? I think too much money is spent on ridiculous things like the Millennium Dome and sculptures in the city centre to make the place look pretty, instead of spending it on education and the NHS.'

(Paula)

'The government has done something for the homeless by providing funding for shelters, but that's not the same as permanent homes.'

(Claire)

'One thing that really annoys me is the amount of money that some people are paid, like nurses, when you see pop stars going out and getting millions of pounds for one advert, or football players who might only play for a couple of minutes of the match and still get paid thousands of pounds. Some football players are getting £50,000–£60,000 a week and a nurse wouldn't earn that in four years. I don't see how anybody kicking a pig's bladder around the place should get paid more than somebody who saves lives. This pay differential and the way the world values different people is ludicrous. We should all be ashamed.'

(Darron)

'I'd like to do something about famine and suffering in places like Ethiopia. Imagine if you've got nothing and you have to walk a million miles just for a bit of water. We sit here and we've got loads of luxuries that we take for granted. I did a 24-hour sponsored fast and we had to go and sit in McDonalds one Saturday and watch everyone else stuffing their faces with Big Macs whilst we couldn't. The sponsor money went to help World Vision provide clean water in Africa. When you think about it afterwards, you've done such a little thing and anybody could do it and it would help so much if everyone did it.'

(Sarah)

'Even if you do give, it's not very much really. You see those little boxes on counters in shops where you can put your change, but it's nothing really. It's strange how all of us are human beings, yet some of us have just got so much, whilst some people have got absolutely nothing in some parts of the world. Why does the majority of the world's population live in poverty, and the rest complain that they can't afford a bigger car? It's all about greed really when you think about it. People just want more and more and more. I think this is the greatest failing of the human race.'

(Jayne)

'What you need to do is have a maximum wage that people could have, so that any money you earned or came to you on top of that, would have to go to other people, to charity, or whatever. You look at Africa and all the people that are suffering in some of the countries out there; then you look at us and see people who are earning hundreds of thousands of pounds a year. They really don't need that much money, so it should stop somewhere and the extra should go to help things balance out a bit more. Instead of making the rich richer, time and energy should be spent on balancing out the financial inequalities across the globe.'

(Robert)

'What is strange is that people will pay £1 a week because they think there's a chance they might win the lottery jackpot, which is ten million pounds or so. Then you look at Comic Relief which might raise £20 million over weeks and weeks with thousands of people putting in massive effort. If everybody thinks £1 a week is an insignificant amount to just throw away on the lottery, why don't they give £1 a week to charity from what they earn? The lottery money is just redistributed around Great Britain. so it's not doing anything for the country. Lots of people get a little bit poorer and some people get a lot richer. If everyone forgot about the lottery because the chances of winning it are so remote anyway and put that £1 into a charity box, you'd know it would be going to a good cause.'

(Alastair)

'You could set up a fund for all the unexpected and unpredictable disasters like floods, hurricanes and such like. You don't know when they're going to happen and people need resources to build up their lives again and receive emergency food and water. Maybe if the extra money the rich people have got went into a disaster fund, that would be a much better situation than what we have at the moment. One person doesn't need the kind of huge wins that you get with the lottery, especially when you have a rollover and a possible prize win of £14 million. It needs to be shared out more. Doesn't one of the world religions have a rule that means you have to give a percentage of your annual income to charity, which I think is a really good idea? I think the government should make it compulsory, by law, for people who earn over a certain amount to give a percentage of their income to the less fortunate.'

(Sarah)

'I'd like to do something about homelessness. People don't really want to live out on the streets.'

(Lisa)

'I'm not being horrible to my mum, but she sits and watches the lottery and she says, "Please let me win, please let me win", and when she finds out she hasn't won she says, "Oh, God, I could have done with some of that." But my mum doesn't need more money. We've got a nice house; we've got plenty of clothes; we've got enough food. We don't need more money.'

(Audrey)

'We're all greedy. We sit in our comfy homes wanting more money, whilst other people have nothing. You feel frustrated because all you need is another tenner to get those trainers, or a fiver to get that CD. You're thinking, All I need is a bit more money, whilst there are people out there who are actually dying.'

(Paul)

'The problem is knowing where to start, because there are so many problems in the world and so many factors that affect one's priorities. Often people don't actually know how they could be helping.'

(Amelia)

'I'd like to do something about racism. It's not enough for parliament to make a law and say people can't be racist. It's harder than that. You have to start doing something from an early age.'

(Jendayi)

'There's countries fighting over who has the tallest building in the world, whilst there are people who don't have homes. That's just selfish.'

(Carly)

# 3

# Comparisons with previous generations

'When I grow up I want to be a teacher in a secondary school. I would like to teach manners. I will have one child to see what they are like, and if I like them, I will have more children. If I cannot be a teacher I will be a pop star.'

Kelly Gill, age 8, in *Our World 2000* (Save the Children 1999)

It is more than thirty years since Edward Blishen edited *The School That I'd Like*, a collection of secondary school pupils' responses to a competition of the same name organized by the *Observer* in December 1967 (Blishen 1969). In that time much has changed with regard to the organization and funding of education. In the early sixties selection through the 11-plus was the accepted system, with 1200 grammar schools in existence throughout the UK. By 2000, only 162 of the 5000 state-funded secondary schools were still grammar schools, and this number may reduce through parental ballots. Selection by aptitude has largely replaced selection by ability in the state sector, although the story is very different in the private sector.

Catering for around 9 per cent of secondary age pupils, the private sector has remained remarkably resilient to the upheavals of the last thirty years. Some of these changes, such as the abolition of 'direct grant' status for 170 grammar schools in 1975 (whose funding came from central government instead of from the local education authority), and the introduction of the 'assisted places' scheme in 1980 (which was subsidizing 34,000 children at its peak in 1996), have served to boost their numbers. With their increasingly selective intake and small classes, independent schools take most of the top 100 places in the A level league tables, and a large share of available places at universities – particularly the select few who describe themselves as the 'Russell group' (Passmore 1999).

In the early days of comprehensive reorganization some grammar schools (including most of the direct grant ones) opted for independence as fee-paying schools, but the majority transformed into the comprehensive schools which are attended by 90 per cent of children across the UK. John Major's election promise of 1997 to commit the Conservative Party to re-establish a 'grammar school in every town' was ridiculed by the majority of the electorate, as well as many from within his own party, including the aspirant who was to replace him as leader. William Hague had turned his back on Ripon Grammar School, preferring the education on offer at the local comprehensive. 'Education, Education, Education' became the catchphrase of both major parties in the 1997 election (the only point of difference being the order of importance!). Emerging victorious, Tony Blair pledged 'to modernize the comprehensive principle'.

The role of Local Education Authorities (LEAs) has also changed. Until 1988 the 104 chief education officers across the country were responsible for almost every aspect of primary, secondary, tertiary and special school provision in their respective areas. Some of these areas were very big indeed, with budgets running into hundreds of millions. The LEA controlled the disbursement of this money to schools and colleges, often taking note of individual circumstances of local schools, some of whom had a high number of challenging pupils and special needs.

Following the 1988 Education Act, with its clauses on Local Management of Schools (LMS), opting out, parental choice and governing bodies, the power of LEAs was curtailed considerably. Several years later 'incorporation' led to the separation of colleges from LEA control, and then local government reorganization in the latter part of the decade saw many of the huge LEAs carved up into smaller regions. The region of Avon for instance, which had contained 60 secondary schools and 350 primary schools in 1995, was divided into five separate districts, most with ten or so rural secondary schools, leaving the director of education in Bristol responsible for a rump of 23 secondary schools, 123 primary schools and 11 special schools, many of them in the heart of the inner city areas.

By 2000 LEAs were required to delegate 90 per cent of their educational budgets directly to schools, leaving them responsible for school meals provision, pupil transport, allocation of school places, and special needs, with an advisory and support and inspectorial function often eroded or superseded by the work of Ofsted (Office for Standards in Education). In some parts of the country chief education officers such as Tim Brighouse were still able to offer leadership and inspiration to teachers working in their area through their own vision and moral authority, but the power to direct change had long gone.

Participation rates have also changed since Edward Blishen's book. In 1967 only 25 per cent of young people continued into the sixth form after O levels, and many of the departing 75 per cent had gone as soon as they were legally able to at 15. Most of them found work quite easily, since unemployment was around 3 per cent of the population. Now the situation is almost completely reversed, with 75 per cent undertaking further education in school sixth forms or colleges of further education (FE) after taking their GCSEs. The minority 25 per cent who leave at 16 often experience difficulty in finding employment of any sort, apart from that which is part-time and low-paid.

1967 was the year of the Plowden Report, *Children and their Primary Schools* (DES 1967), which endorsed the student-centred approach favoured by most teachers. It was also the year of the Abortion Act and the Sexual Offences Act; the year in which Che Guevara was killed and colour television was first broadcast in the UK; the year in which Radio 1 was created and the first heart transplant operation was carried out. In 1967 Edward Blishen's secondary school respondents were critical of the passive experience that characterized the process of schooling:

'Everything learnt is second hand if it comes from teachers, and very often out of date and misleading if it comes from books.'

(Richard, in Blishen 1969: 74)

'Far better to replace constipated ways of teaching with more active lessons, with teachers and pupils discussing.'

(Lynnette, in Blishen 1969: 83)

'I am tired of hearing that the hope of my country lies in my generation. If you give me the same indoctrination as a child how can you expect me to be any different to you?'

v. Society

(Graham, in Blishen 1969: 7)

The majority were in favour of comprehensive schools and against segregation, in favour of assessment of achievement but against an examination system that put a straitjacket on the syllabus or required a one-off act of memorization. They wanted disciplined classrooms, but not against a backdrop of foolish rules which had an explosive effect on the adolescent. They were against homework because they were in favour of time for all that other work that young people are engaged in as leisure activities. They were kind about teachers, although they wanted younger ones and 'would retire them at 35 before crippling old age set in!' Most of them favoured school uniform but wanted a brighter version that reflected current fashion. There was universal antipathy to what was seen as the indoctrination of religious assemblies, feeling it was a failure to grasp an opportunity to 'debate moral issues and affairs of the spirit'.

Standing out above everything else is the children's desire to teach themselves, rather than to be the passive targets of teaching: a great restlessness about classrooms, timetables, the immemorial and so often inert routine of schools. The children seem to sense what their elders are slow to sense, that you enter the world of the late twentieth century ill armed if all you have done is to submit, to some degree or other, to a pre-determined, punched, examination-harried course of instruction, from which in its nature most of the excitement and surprise of learning are excluded. They want to take risks – lord how anxious they are to be at risk, intellectually and emotionally.

(Blishen 1969: 14)

Thirteen years after *The School That I'd Like* was published, I conducted a series of individual interviews with young people around the UK, published as *Tales out of School* (White with Brockington 1983). Almost all of them had left school at 16 and were in work, or were unemployed, or were in the twilight world of semi-employment on the Youth Opportunities programme. They were encouraged to reflect on their eleven years of compulsory schooling. What struck me at the time was that, although most of them had left school with little prospect of further education, all of them had interests, skills and perceptions that made me wonder at the waste of ability. For whatever reason a vast, untapped resource of human potential seemed to have passed through our schools unrecognized.

In one particular and noticeable sense, the 16-year-olds interviewed in the previous chapter are very different to those interviewed for *Tales out of School*. They are succeeding in school and want to continue with their education. They tend to be in the higher sets and are looking forward to a good clutch of GCSE passes. Yet it is interesting to note how similar their comments are to those I'd recorded nearly twenty years ago. Likewise, in contrasting Edward Blishen's school children's comments with those recorded in the previous chapter, the similarities are also striking, although his cohort are now the parents and, in some cases, the grandparents of those interviewed here.

The **transition from primary to secondary school** for instance is still one of the most nerve-wracking experiences that children remember. They move from a junior school environment, where they are well known by staff and parents, and surrounded by long-established friendships, to an environment where they are at the bottom of the pecking order with huge numbers of alien faces around them. In many cases their close friends from primary school transfer to other schools or other classes, and they experience the challenge of making new friendships – something many of them have not had to do since the age of 4. 'You hear lots of rumours about what they are going to do with you,' says Richard, and 'Coming to a school like this seemed so massive. It was really quite frightening,' says Claire on page 12 of this book.

Thirty years ago *The School That I'd Like* (Blishen 1969) contained similar comments:

> 'At present the main difference between secondary and primary school is that primary education is enjoyable and secondary education is absolutely dreary and boring. Primary education . . . that golden land where the revolution has partially taken place. May it soon take place in our secondary schools.'
>
> (Stephen, in Blishen 1969: 36)

> 'In primary schools there is a friendly relationship between teacher and pupil and the children feel at ease with their teacher. Do not try and improve on this; you may spoil it!'
>
> (Jane, in Blishen 1969: 36)

And *Tales out of School* (White with Brockington 1983) recorded the following:

'When you went to secondary school for the first day a big gang of kids would come round and knock the shit out of you; up till I left that was the ruling. You got your trousers or jumper ripped as some sort of initiation to the school.'

(Gordon, in White with Brockington 1983: 17)

'There was a load of difference. When you were at junior school, the teachers would come and sit by you. They'd watch you writing and they'd have discussions with you. In secondary schools they just didn't involve themselves like that.'

(John, in White with Brockington 1983: 15)

It is small wonder that they are apprehensive about this period of transition, and how the fears can be so easily fuelled by those who conjure with stories of bullying and induction rites that hark back to *Tom Brown's Schooldays*.

For myself and many of those of my generation that started secondary schooling in the early sixties, such fears were justified. At the age of 10 I flew back from Singapore to Stansted in a propeller-assisted Britannia of the Royal Air Force to start at a boarding school in the south of England. It was a common experience for many 'service children' whose fathers had been posted abroad to one of the outposts of the fast-diminishing Empire. I travelled the 9000 miles on my own and was met at Stansted by two elderly friends of my parents whose task was to kit me out in the appropriate uniform and deliver me to my new school at the allotted hour. In my first week at school I had several experiences reminiscent of Tom Brown, including being lightly roasted in front of the common room fire as a punishment for running up the unlit path from the prep room to the dining room. I was scared of the dark and, although it was less than 50 yards from one room to another, the swaying bushes beside the path hid numerous monsters and terrors. For Nicholls, the 17-year-old prefect who apprehended me, this was an excellent opportunity to instil some discipline into one of the 'new bugs'.

Later that week Nicholls took further delight in winning the competition to be the first prefect to 'cosh the virgin arses' of myself and the other four new bugs that shared a dormitory. Our crime was to be caught talking after 'lights out'.

Nicholls and others like him were one of the reasons why the transition to secondary schooling was so intimidating in the early sixties. But in this respect things have certainly changed since Blishen's days. Secondary schools lay on taster days for their partner primary schools to help with the selection of school and to allay fears of the unknown. Most secondary schools give the new intake time in the school on their own before the returning cohorts of older pupils overwhelm them with their energy and presence. Mentoring schemes are in place in many schools, where sixth formers are paired up with new pupils to guide and support them through their first term. Care is taken with the choice of tutors and the construction of each tutor group, to help pupils form friendships that will sustain them through their time in school.

And *friendships* are clearly so significant for young people. It is this ingredient that can make or mar the enjoyment of being in secondary school. It is crucial to have friends, to be accepted as part of a group, to know you belong, and so crushing for those children left on the outside, or the butt for bullying children. The 16-year-old pupils interviewed in the previous chapter speak eloquently about this aspect of schooling. There is no doubt that those secondary schools who regard the nurturing of friendships and the tackling of bullying as a priority will be allaying a major worry for children that has resonated for years through our system of education, as the following comments from *Tales out of School* indicate.

> 'My best friend went to a different school and I was split up from my other friends, because we were put in classes according to how clever we were. I was in the top class but I never fitted in because I still went around with my old friends at play time – so I was sort of singled out by people in my class.'
>
> (Andrew, in White with Brockington 1983: 16)

> 'The worst part of it was changing classes and changing teachers. In primary school you get addicted to one teacher and you can say, "Right, I'll see so and so tomorrow"; same old thing every day. But in secondary school there are so many different rooms, so many different people and so many kids. It's like going to Wembley I suppose. If you need help, if something's difficult, or a load of people ask you a question and you don't know, they start giving you the elbow and start taking the piss. You get called all sorts of names if you have trouble and you can't do it.'
>
> (Matthew, in White with Brockington 1983: 15)

Ten years later Keele University's Centre for Successful Schools undertook a research programme which used a questionnaire survey to investigate attitudes of over 30,000 young people about all aspects of secondary schooling (Barber 1994). Responses came from pupils in a wide range of schools and, although Michael Barber was careful to point out the limitations of the research, they echo many of the points made by the classes of 1969 and 1983, such as the concerns about bullying (see Barber 1997: 77).

> 'Bullying is the worst thing about the school. Before you start you are promised that if anyone does bully you, steps will be taken. This is not

true. A group of us were bullied right up to the third year and we were just told to stay away from them. They were not stopped, even when one of us was hit . . . The headmaster just tries to ignore the issue.'

'What I don't like is that because I'm fat, people call me names and take the mickey and I get scared, and because I'm big they want to beat me up because they think I'm a good challenge.'

'Overall pupils at this school are pleasant to know but there appears to be a disturbing amount of racism, mostly against Asian members of the school.'

'It is difficult to find happiness because there are lots of bullying people in this school.'

'I feel so scared when the fourth years push you out of the way when you bump into them by accident and when they start having a go and everybody crowds round . . . they say how I stink and my legs are so skinny and they cuss my mum.'

These sorts of comments were echoed by many respondents to the Industrial Society's (1997) survey of almost 10,000 young people. Entitled *Speaking Up Speaking Out*, the summative report printed a number of these to illustrate the extent of the problem.

'They pushed me on the bench and my tooth broke. And bashed my head and different things like that . . . I thought "tell them to stop doing that" but I kept it to myself. I didn't want to say anything.'
(19-year-old from Sussex, in Industrial Society 1997: 206)

'I have been bullied . . . It's mostly verbal, which is actually more hurtful than physical. It actually puts you in more of a state than just getting punched. If they call you something, you can't prove it and you just get really upset about it because they can always do that again . . . I've been bullied ever since I was in school, from when I was in primary up to now. But it's actually gone down quite a lot because people have realised you can't cast me down because I am gay. People still go past me and say "He's queer", but I mean, so what? I am, but that's not going to hurt me in the least really.'
(15-year-old from London, in Industrial Society 1997: 206)

'The school I went to was racist . . . and they didn't accept me for what I was; like the kids there didn't understand me, because me and my sisters were the only black people in that school and they didn't understand why no one explained it properly, so they took it upon themselves that we were different and we always were going to be different.'
(16-year-old from Birmingham, in Industrial Society 1997: 207)

In the previous chapter Ryan makes a very telling point on page 21 when he says, 'Having friends is really important, so that you can stand up for each other when you need some help.' Alongside this emphasis on the significance of being with friends and concerns about how they will be treated by other pupils, the students say a lot about the importance of the teacher. Edward Blishen's contributors filled many pages on *teachers* and what made for *good teaching*, as did those interviewed for *Tales out of School* (White with Brockington 1983), the Keele University Survey (Barber 1994), and *Speaking Up, Speaking Out* (Industrial Society 1997).

'Teachers should be enthusiastic about their subject. There is nothing worse than sitting in a lesson knowing full well that the teacher is dying to get rid of you and rush back to the staff room to have her cup of tea.'

(Jeremy, in Blishen 1969: 141)

'There is no substitute for the infectious human element of a teacher deeply in love with his subject. He alone will set fire to my soul. I need guidance to mould my chalky dreams into a rich and satisfying adulthood. My need is now, today. Tomorrow is somewhere else.'

(Susan, in Blishen 1969: 20)

'Schools would not be schools without teachers. Those great beings so full of knowledge, wisdom . . . and old age. People say the older you are the wiser you are. They forget the older you are the less patient you become with youth – that noisy bunch of hooligans who insist on running in the corridors and scribbling "United for the Cup" and "I love Steve" on the blackboard.'

(Jennifer, in Blishen 1969: 137)

'The best teachers are those who aren't trying to project their authority all the time – who feel secure in allowing you to go so far and no further.'

(Nicola, in White with Brockington 1983: 47)

'The way teachers start lessons is important. If the minute you get in there they shout at you, you think, Oh, Christ, here we go. If you go to talk to somebody and it's "Oi, shut up!" that's when it boils up inside you.'

(Matthew, in White with Brockington 1983: 48)

'You don't think of them as people. It sounds hard to believe – kids thinking that teachers aren't people – but that's how it is. If you saw them down town or something you couldn't believe it. You used to say, "Oh look, it's Mrs So and So" and stand there amazed, especially if they'd said "hello" to you.'

(Mandy, in White with Brockington 1983: 58)

'Teachers need to learn psychology, learn about the mind and how to motivate it, so that they can create a sort of lust for knowledge in the classroom . . . If you teach a subject by making children memorise facts you might as well be a tape recorder. The crucial thing is being able to motivate children.'

(TC, in White with Brockington 1983: 59)

'Some of the teachers in my school give you the impression that you're stupid when you ask them to explain more than once.'

(Barber 1997: 80)

'I feel it is important that teachers listen to what we have to say as usually we have something useful or important to say.'

(in Barber 1997: 80)

'Teachers favour the more intelligent students in our class and don't help us less intelligent students enough.'

(in Barber 1997: 80)

'My maths teacher's brilliant, she's amazing, it's incredible the way she teaches it; it's just so clear and everything just fits into place; I never understood maths could be so simple. Generally we are regarded by the teachers as people, which I hear is unusual.'

(Girl from London, in Industrial Society 1997: 200)

'A boy in my class he really spent ages on this piece of work . . . he got it wrong, but he did his best handwriting and everything on his maths homework, and his teacher said that he had to do it again, and she didn't even compliment him on how neat it was. He's left handed and it's very hard to write and he doesn't write very well.'

(Boy from Essex, in Industrial Society 1997: 204)

'I felt the teachers were very good, the quality was good . . . we did everything the hearing children would do. We followed a proper curriculum.'

(Young man from London, in Industrial Society 1997: 201)

In the section on 'Learning and Education', *Speaking Up Speaking Out* noted that young people want to learn in an environment that values young people's achievements and in which teachers are committed and approachable, and boost young people's confidence and enthusiasm. Teachers, rather than facilities, class sizes or subject options were considered to be the most important factors in creating a 'good' school.

Other contemporary studies have focused on this issue. Jean Rudduck's edited collection *School Improvement: What Can Pupils Tell Us?* (1996), Chris Kyriacou's *Essential Teaching Skills* (1998), and Colin Morgan and Glyn Morris's *Good Teaching and Learning* (1999) further illuminate what young people value about teachers.

Our argument in this book is that what pupils say about teaching, learning and schooling is not only worth listening to but provides an important foundation for thinking about ways of improving schools. Our broad summary of what pupils have told us in interview is that whilst teachers are for the most part supportive, stimulating and selfless in the hours they put in to help young people, the conditions of learning that are common across secondary schools do not adequately take account of the social maturity of young people.

(Rudduck 1996)

Good rapport comes from conveying to pupils that you understand, share and value their perspective as individuals on a whole range of matters and experiences, academic, social and personal: for example, expressing sympathy when the local football team gets knocked out of the cup competition, praise for a pupil who has performed well in a school play, concern for a pupil who has a bad cold, and excitement that a school trip is near.

(Kyriacou 1998)

In this chapter pupils send very clear messages about what constitutes good teaching. It pre-eminently is to do with the quality of the teacher's methods of presentation, range of learning activities, explanation and giving of feedback, classroom control and order, and interpersonal relationships. 'Quality teaching' for pupils is about activity, not passivity; about negotiation and close relationships, not distance and deference.

(Morgan 1999)

Such comments about the importance of the interaction with teachers are echoed by those young people interviewed for this book. It is clear that relationships with teachers significantly affect their attitudes to learning, a point reinforced by Michael Rutter and his team in their book *Fifteen Thousand Hours* more than twenty years ago. They were searching for the elusive qualities that seemed to account for differences in performance between schools with similar intakes. Those that took relationships between pupils and staff very seriously – where there was strong emphasis on extra-curricular activities – demonstrated better examination results. 'We found very few measures of the extent of shared activity between staff and pupils, but it was found that schools in which a high proportion of children had been on out of school outings had better academic outcomes' (Rutter 1979: 196).

In a climate where the national curriculum dominates the timetable construction, it is important to note that involvement in **extra-curricular activities** can often be a factor that enhances performance in school subjects. This is something that teachers of music, PE, drama have known for years and is borne out by an analysis of research studies into the effects of music teaching, carried out by the Campaign for Music in the Curriculum. *The Fourth R: The Case for Music in the Curriculum* (1998) provided evidence for improved performance in reading, mathematics, science and engineering, enhanced fluency in speaking languages, and heightened capabilities for reasoning and problem solving. The *TES* made much of these findings in a special feature:

> Impressive results came from Switzerland's two year 'music makes the school' project, which involved 1200 children from 50 classes. It discovered that those given extra music lessons proved better at reading and languages than those pupils in the control groups. They were also more sociable, better motivated and more relaxed.
>
> (Spencer 1998)

By 2000 the Campaign for Music had initiated a research project involving 400 6- and 7-year-olds in seven primary schools in the London Borough of Newham. The purpose was to compare the achievement and behaviour of one class that had 15 minutes of music every day with that of another class that received normal lessons. Paradoxically, time spent on music and away from 'academic' work may actually improve academic attainment (Dean 2000).

The discovery by researchers at Durham University in 1999 that those primary school children who did less, rather than more, homework actually performed better in SATs tests is a similar sort of paradox, which challenges some of our basic presuppositions about learning. It seems not to make sense. The less you do the better you perform. Not surprisingly their research findings were lambasted by many from an educational establishment that regards endeavour as a key determinant of success (Bunting 1999). The two perspectives appear to be in conflict, but there may actually be some common ground, especially if consideration is given to what children are doing when they're doing 'less' homework.

As anyone who has consciously learnt anything knows, you can make faster progress by interspersing your focused practice with some completely different activities. Indeed there is a point at which you seem to go backwards unless you take a break. Whenever I pick up my guitar and stumble through chords and notes to a point where I can play a recognizable tune, it is noticeable that I soon reach a point where the more I try to play well, the worse my playing gets. Yet if I put the guitar down, make a cup of tea, sit in the sun for a bit, and return to the guitar half an hour later, there is a surprising advance made in the interval when I've not been playing the guitar.

How many times have you given up struggling with what seems like an intractable problem, gone to bed to sleep on it, and awoken in the morning with the solution crystal clear in your mind? These apparent paradoxes can be explained in a number of ways such as left brain–right brain polarities, or by a consideration of Gardner's intelligences (see page 82) and the inter-play between aspects of our intellectual make-up, or by studies into 'deep' and 'surface' learning. All work and no play makes Jack a dull boy. The Greeks and Romans knew it too: *'mens sana in corpore sano'*. It is one of the explanations for the phenomenal success of the Award Scheme Devel-opment and Accreditation Network (ASDAN) programmes in schools, where time spent on cultural, recreational and interpersonal activities actually has a knock-on benefit on academic performance (ASDAN 2000).

It is the value of 'chatting with a friend', the occasional joke between teacher and class, or the digression from the specific topic that young peo-ple are acknowledging as significant in these remarks. *'Education is what happens when a good teacher gets off the point'* wrote Nicholas Gillett in 1978, a sentiment endorsed twenty years later by Andrew Cunningham, an English teacher, in an article for the *TES* headed 'Brilliance that cannot be inspected':

> Playing safe with stodgy syllabuses and microscopic schemes of work is an anathema to the brilliant teacher. He or she knows what makes kids tick can't be reduced to attainment targets. They want fizz, fun and sparkle. And they want to be taught by teachers capable of deliver-ing that heady cocktail . . . The curriculum should remain sacrosanct: a pool of infinite possibilities for each teacher to tap into. Until we reaffirm our faith in brilliance, the future for beaks looks bleak.
>
> (Cunningham 1999: 21)

Reading through the comments of the class of 1999, there is clearly much that they feel positive about in relation to school, although they are as critical of the resources available and the state of school buildings as were Edward Blishen's children thirty years ago.

> 'It's all very odd. We have a brand new language laboratory, with a film projector affair which shows cartoons with French commentary on a TV screen, but our textbooks are falling to pieces. We have sev-eral large science laboratories that are clean enough to perform brain surgery in, while our lavatories are minus chains or minus doorlocks or minus toilet paper, or minus all three'
>
> (Elen, in Blishen 1969: 47)

> 'Dear Lord, please give us a school which is cool in summer and warm enough in winter for us to sit without coats and gloves. Let there be an end to these dreary places where the sun never penetrates, where only one small window opens, though the rest admit small gales, where the draughts howl through the sacred portals and where the electric light is on constantly from November till April. And might we also have lavatories which do not freeze up in cold weather?'
>
> (Anne, in Blishen 1969: 17)

The ambivalence about *school uniform* is still there, although it would seem that, if there has been any shift at all, it is towards a position more in favour of uniform. As well as acknowledging that it goes some way towards disguising poverty, they are also conscious that it saves them having to compete with other children in the fashion stakes, and cuts down on the number of critical decisions that have to be made between tumbling out of bed and leaving the house to head for school. 'If I didn't have a uniform, I'd wake up in the morning and think, Oh my God, what am I going to wear?' says Lisa on page 24.

What shines out from the pages in the final section is a deep concern about *inequality and injustice* and the contribution that school can make to exploring these issues. The concerns of the class of 1999 echo those of former generations of school children.

'When we look at our schools today and politicians say we've got one of the best educational systems in the world, we realise how low standards must be. In my ideal school the pupils would talk freely about religion, politics, music, sport or whatever else they wished to discuss. It would be a place where the pupils would be learning to live with each other and with "outsiders" . . . It would be a place where people learn to reason, learn to understand and above all learn to think for themselves. School was not invented just for the little people to become the same as the big people.'

(Judith, in Blishen 1969: 30)

'Knowledge of nuclear physics and the ability to write a treatise on the abolition of slavery might be very interesting in itself, but it does not come up in everyday conversation very frequently, neither does it equip one to run a home and look after a family. I think the reading of modern and not obscure novels, the appreciation of contemporary art and ideas on how to furnish a room and live on a few pounds a week would be more useful.'

(Carolynne, in Blishen 1969: 83)

'Communication is very, very important . . . talking is one way of breaking down prejudices, like between black and white. If you can encourage black people to talk with whites, tell them about themselves so that whites get to know them, you can begin to break down the prejudice that their parents have drummed into them. The trouble is it needs schools to be more open places but they tend to teach you to be competitive. You're not really taught to share, but when you leave school and live with someone, you have to share. Being taught to keep things to yourself, like saying "This is my work, you can't copy it," doesn't help you. Doing things in groups would make it better. People say it's not natural to share things, but if you're married you're sharing with the person you're married to. Anyway people do share a lot of things, like shops and roads for example!'

(Jo, in White with Brockington 1983: 19)

'Most thirteen year olds don't make it to the sixth form and don't get used to making decisions – yet two years after leaving school they can vote. Somehow they have to get used to making decisions. Youth clubs could help out in this way. They should be more than just leisure centres. With their relaxed atmosphere they could take a more active role in teaching kids decision making. Schools can't cover everything from nine to three thirty.'

(Leslie, in White with Brockington 1983: 21)

When Leslie made that comment in the early eighties, it was true that most young people didn't make it into the sixth form. In that sense a great deal has changed. Two-thirds of young people are now in full-time education or training at the age of 17, which may reflect structural shifts in the job market and the kind of work on offer to 16-year-olds as much as interest in continuing education, although aspirations and expectations have certainly changed in relation to higher education.

Currently, around half of each sixth form cohort will go on to higher education – that is about 35 per cent of the entire age group. The remainder will mostly go straight into employment at 17 or 18, and a good number of these will continue with further training. Compared to ten or twenty years ago this is a remarkable improvement and reflects changes that have taken place at all levels of the system as Tim Brighouse highlighted in his Moray House Lecture in 1999:

Ten years ago only 18 per cent of Birmingham children achieved five or more A*–C grades: now the figure is 38 per cent. In the same period the national improvement is from 37 per cent to 47 per cent, just 10 per cent. We are catching up. Five years ago only 35 per cent of youngsters at eleven were at, or above, their chronological age in reading; now 65 per cent are. Maths is even more of a success story. Indeed 40 youngsters this summer in one primary school took and obtained GCSE. But it is the march of the inevitable that bolsters my confidence. When my mum, who is 94, left school only 0.5 per cent received higher education; when I left school 3 per cent did. When my eldest child left in 1981 the figure was 12 per cent; now it is 30–35 per cent. The strongest determinant of a child's success is a mother's level of education. By 2020 the percentage entering higher education will be 60 per cent and a higher figure for women. By then we shall have put some distance between education and catastrophe as Wells put it. Our successors will kindly wonder at the limit of our expectations and the modesty of our reach.

(Brighouse 1999)

Tim Brighouse is right to be celebratory and to draw attention to one of the factors that has been most significant in achieving this remarkable change – the quality of the teaching profession. Yet, at the same time, we need to be aware that the gap between those in different socioeconomic groups has been widening steadily. The report in November 1999 entitled *Access for All – A Survey of Post-16 Participation* (Commons Education and Employment Select Committee 1999) exposes the increasing differential between the 'haves' and the 'have-nots', and the worryingly low number of those in lower socioeconomic groups who stay on beyond the compulsory age. Government policies such as Sure Start and Excellence in Cities are intended to address this and David Blunkett comments more on these in Chapter 7.

Meanwhile, the next two chapters concentrate on the comments of sixth formers – the two-thirds of the age group that now continue into what is described as 'post-compulsory education'. Many of their remarks echo those of their 16-year-old compatriots and, as their sights become more focused on university entrance or the world of work, they extend the debate into other areas.

## 4

# Past and present: comments from sixth formers

**On the benefits of going to school . . .**

'Gaining confidence through involvement in extra-curricular activities. I'm back stage manager for a production. I go on trips with the school, like skiing. It's the other things that help widen your experience I suppose.'

(Peter)

'A lot of the extra-curricular activities I've got involved with through school have given me more confidence. I did the Institute of Management Challenge at school, where you have to work on a problem and make a presentation at the end about what you've done. The presentation has to be made in front of people you don't know, and that gave me a lot more confidence because I really didn't think I could do it.'

(Clare)

'The staff here have a genuine interest in your well being, in you doing well. Many people are in jobs where they are just doing a job, but you get the sense that the teachers here enjoy what they're doing. At different times, some of us have had problems with different teachers. But the final outcome is what you see now with us. It's like something went through the mill and something totally different came out. We've grown up. I think we are like adults now, so most of our mature growing stage has been in this school. That's a tribute to what we have become through the school.'

(Keji)

'Your confidence grows as you move up the school. When you're in Year 7 you're all shy because it's a new school, new friends, new teachers. But as you get into Year 11 the teachers become more like friends. Your confidence grows. You don't just learn at school. You become more mature. You take on more responsibilities.'

(Alison)

'The best things have been the effect on friendships and personality. In the past two or three years my confidence has been boosted and I'm not so shy as I used to be ten years ago. Without school these things wouldn't have developed. I've been helped by the fact that the school has many high-quality teachers. I haven't yet come across a teacher who didn't seem to know what they were talking about. They are all extremely helpful and committed to their subjects.'

(David)

'It's a great opportunity to learn new things. Primary school was OK, but here you can really study some things in depth. I find that exciting. I've had some brilliant teachers who made me want to find out more about their subjects. I've nearly always looked forward to coming to school.'

(Lisa)

'School is full of experiences; it's not just the learning.'

(Donna)

'It gives you a chance to integrate with other people and develop social relationships and learn things about other people that you can't within a family. You mix with people the same age as you and you mix with people of authority who aren't your parents, so you develop relationships unlike those within the family. It's very important to have a different relationship with your parents than other people in authority.'

(Nicola)

'You encounter different influences. You come across different opinions to your own. You learn from other people. You refine your own opinions by listening to other people's opinions and their experiences. It's part of being in a school. It gives you an opportunity to find out and understand what works for you; which is a really important lesson for life. You discover how to be self-motivated.'

(Lizzie)

'In theory schools provide children, no matter what their background or religious preference, with a safe environment in which to learn, develop and grow. They should give everyone the same chance to develop the unspoken skills that aren't recognized on an exam certificate: skills such as social interaction, appreciation of others, and a recognition of the complexity of relationships.'

(Karen)

'Education is about picking up social skills, listening to authority, learning how to learn, working out what you really think about things, as well as learning actual subjects like maths and English and so on.'

(Nick)

'Going to school is the first time you've been away from mum or dad or parental guidance and, although you're set guidelines, it's the first opportunity for you to get out on your own and make your own friends and relationships.'

(Leon)

'It's an opportunity to learn about the hierarchy of relationships, authority and things like that, which prepares you for what it's going to be like when you step out into the world. When you first go to primary school you take along all the opinions about life from your parents. You learn about all the different cultures and what people are like, so you're building up your own personality as you go through school, so that when you come out of school at 18 you know what kind of individual you really are. You know what you like, what sort of people you like, who your friends are, what type of subjects you are going to do, what kind of job you want to do.'

(Laura)

'It's a big socializing pot. You have so many different people from different backgrounds and families. Being in school is like putting them into a big pot and stirring them all around. You find out how other people are brought up, what their families are like, and it all influences you. The trouble is, not everyone's in the pot, because some people go to private schools.'

(Katy)

'I've enjoyed the fact that there's good relationships between pupil and teacher. It gets better the longer you stay in school, especially if you get involved with things like the school play. Things are much friendlier these days. That's probably one of the main advantages of getting rid of corporal punishment. If the teacher's got the power to hit you, you're not going to have the same sort of relationship. It's also good to mix with lots of other people. When I play football, I make friends with people in my year that I wouldn't normally mix with. If I'm in the school play it involves pupils from up and down the school. When you're younger, you look up to the older actors; then when you're older, you give the younger kids a hand, show them how it's done and calm their nerves. It's good fun.'

(Karim)

'We have had the opportunity to experience other cultures. Although you can learn about them in lessons, unless you really experience them, for yourself, you are only aware of your own culture. Going abroad gives you the opportunity to experience a different way of life and understand attitudes of people who live completely different lives. It enables you to reflect on what you have at home and helps you make decisions about what you want to do with your life and where you want to be. Putting yourself in a situation you find hard develops you as a person.'

(Jennifer)

'I've had the opportunity to be involved in all sorts of things, apart from just academic subjects. I've enjoyed the atmosphere in the school and my ability to communicate has developed as I've come up through the school. I've felt worthwhile at school, but I'm aware that not everyone feels that. Some people are afraid to commit to extra-curricular activities and just believe their subjects come first.'

(Kirk)

'It's polishing up your communication skills. You have to communicate with lots of different people; learn how to get on with adults as well as children. It's also an opportunity to make lots of friends, because you meet loads of new people. It's all to do with confidence really.'

(Victoria)

'It's about meeting new people, meeting new friends. You're going to have those friends for quite a long time and keep in contact with some of them through university.'

(Joshua)

## On comparisons with previous levels of schooling . . .

'It's much better than any other years. You get your free periods, you get your studies, you're able to specialize in what you're interested in. You're more grown-up. Teachers are more open and talk more. They trust us.'

(Peter)

'We're treated far more as grown-ups, treated more as equals by teachers now we are in the sixth form.'

(Lizzie)

'You're treated differently when you're in the sixth form. The teachers are not as strict with you as they were in lower school. Doing A levels opens your mind. Take maths for instance: you'll be taught things you never knew were there. Say you're in Year 11 and you walk into the maths room and you see the blackboard – you'd just think that was gibberish. You wouldn't know what was going on. But understanding such concepts helps to open your mind more.'

(Manmit)

'I've said to Manmit a few times, "Just think about the amount of knowledge we have in our brains. When you go to university, you're going to have all that medical knowledge in your head and I'm going to have all this accounting knowledge in my head." And that's just the academic knowledge. There's also the non-academic knowledge that you gain from the atmosphere in the school.'

(Keji)

'You start to become the person you are – from interaction with your peers and all the other people around you. Your parents are primary socialization. At this age it's through the school and your friends that you start becoming the person that you become when you leave.'

(Jannine)

'You are treated differently by teachers. They treat you like adults. They're more helpful; their attitude completely changes towards you. They are more like somebody you can depend on as a friend rather than a teacher.'

(Simon)

'I used to see school as something that you had to do. I didn't really appreciate why I was going to school. I used to count the days till the holidays and try to do well in my exams to keep my dad quiet. In the sixth form I'm doing it for me, doing it for myself, not to impress anyone else.'

(Alex M.)

'You get more freedom in the sixth form. You begin to realize that what you're doing is a bit more important, because you've had your first set of real results that can affect the rest of your life really. "Could have done better." And you suddenly start picking up effortwise. Also, I'm doing subjects I enjoy: maths, physics and chemistry. I don't see it so much as hard work. I see it as a challenge, but I don't see it as a labour. You actually want to do well at them because you know it's going to make a difference in the long run.'

(Nawaz)

'I found the difference between Year 11 and sixth form was greater than the difference between primary and secondary school. You're becoming adult. Before, with the teachers, you knew so much less than them. But as you gain in knowledge, you can ask questions. You're getting closer to the teachers and they respect a lot more what you say and what you do.'

(Alex D.)

'You get to know the teachers more as individuals, because you only see three or four of them maybe. You appreciate them as people.'

(Andrew)

'You have to work on your own quite a lot with regard to assignments and research, and, as you go up the school, you have to take on more responsibilities, like prefect duty and community service.'

(Donna)

'It can be difficult not having a uniform. When you're in Year 7 you don't have to worry about what other people said about what you were wearing, because it was basically all the same. However, when you get into Year 12, it's like, "Well, I've got to have that, because if I don't everybody's going to judge me." It's easier for boys because they wear trousers and a shirt, but there are so many different sort of clothes that girls can wear. You can have names said against you if somebody doesn't like the particular clothing you're wearing. So there's a kind of a pressure to wear fashionable clothes – or at least the same sort of clothes that your friends are wearing.'

(Alison)

## On sixth form colleges . . .

'It's good to have sixth form colleges. You come to a new place and meet new people and make loads of new friends. It also develops your confidence. I've made so many friends here and it's made me feel really confident about what I'm going to do next. I think that maybe schools want sixth forms for the wrong reasons, like for the funding or the prestige. I think separate sixth forms are effective in instilling independence in people and pushing people to make individual choice. Sixth form colleges are good at providing a stepping stone between school and university.'

(Katherine)

'I wanted to get away from being labelled as going to secondary school. I didn't mind being around younger people, but I think when you're 16 it's good to move on to somewhere like a college. You're an adult and they treat you like an adult.'

(Phil)

'The atmosphere in the college is open and friendly, and you're given more responsibility for your own learning, which is good. If you don't do the work, there's no-one else to blame! I don't think you are likely to get such an open approach in a school sixth form, which is a shame, because it can leave you quite unprepared for university. One problem

though is that it's expensive to travel here – particularly if your parents are unemployed. The council do give grants and free bus passes, but not to everyone, and there's many more expenses than the council like to believe. There's resources and materials you need for the course, plus all the expenses of being a student together with other students. You need to be able to go to the café, have a drink, those sorts of things. It's all part of being at college.'

(Mark)

'I think sixth form colleges are better than school sixth forms, because teachers are able to be more focused and directed towards specific goals. The change of social groups is a good thing too; personal skills can be more effectively developed when you mix with new people. Also the mature environment and attitude of sixth form colleges promotes concentrated learning, and resources can be used more effectively.'

(Jaclyn)

'The attitude of teachers in this sixth form college is different. In schools they tend to have a patronizing attitude to pupils, like wanting you to call them "Miss". But in this college it's a lot more relaxed and they treat you like adults. Attitudes of the students are different too. In the sixth form in my school, it tended to be people from middle-class backgrounds. In this college, which is the sixth form for the whole of the city, you've got all types of people from different ethnic backgrounds and all different social backgrounds, people that are dressed differently and act differently. There's less bullying.'

(Tanya)

'The other good thing is that they don't remember you when you're 11, because they didn't teach you when you were 11. People see you differently, so you can make a new start. If you didn't do enough work in your school and just achieved C grades, and you'd got a reputation as a slacker, you can start afresh here and say, "Well, I'm not going to do that here; I'm going to do some proper work." Certain people won't do well at sixth form colleges though, because they need a stricter regime to help push them on. It's less of a link to university if you stay on in school. In a school, teachers will say, "You haven't done this work – I'd like the work now", instead of, "You haven't done the work; it's up to you."'

(Matthew)

'Most people want to go to university after they've done their A levels and finished in the sixth form, and it's like the next step, because it's in between school and university. The downside is that it's up to you to bring yourself here and do the work. If you don't, then it's only you that's going to suffer, not the teachers. On the whole people act more maturely here than they did at school. You just seem to grow up really quickly as soon as you get here because you are treated as an adult.'

(Jody)

## On teachers . . .

'Subjects can be brought alive by the teacher. History here is just brilliant. The teacher just made it seem really clear and really interesting. You start asking questions because you want to know why things happened; you want to know more about things. For instance, we were doing rebellions and the history teachers had taken time out to make a game – to show us where the troops were coming from. They'd made a massive map and they brought in little soldiers and we spent a whole lesson moving them around. It was brilliant fun. People were saying afterwards, "That was a really good lesson; I actually learned something. I could visually understand what he'd been trying to explain to us in that lesson." Whereas in the previous lesson he'd just spoken in front of the class and people's minds were just blank. It's good to really live history sometimes, instead of just listening to it.'

(Katherine)

'A good teacher is someone you can have a laugh with, whilst you're learning something. Let's face it, if you don't like the teacher, you're not going to like the lesson, are you? But you do need discipline.'

(Judy)

'You've got to have a sense of humour, but you can't want the pupils to love you. You've just got to be a naturally, interesting, funny person. There are some teachers who aren't particularly inspiring, but who are very well organized. There are others who are very interesting, very good in the classroom, but you don't end up with particularly good notes at the end of the year. So you've got to be organized yourself.'

(Karim)

'Some teachers just won't let you have the time of day. That's not on. You should be treated equally. We don't look at teachers and go, "Right, we like you, but we don't like *you*." It's all to do with how they treat you. You're going to do the same back to them, aren't you? Some teachers think that because we come from this city, we're all just scum.'

(Gary)

'I think you really need to make sure that everyone has time for an individual tutorial at regular intervals so as to review your progress. You have such a short length of time here and you're just one in a class of 25 or 30 people. There's so many people and everyone's at different stages and wants different things. It's really hard for someone to actually get an answer to the particular question that they want answered.'

(Nicola)

'There's a need to feel that there's someone there who is definitely supporting us all the way. I don't mean that we need to be pushed all the time, or that the responsibility for our learning shouldn't be our own, but sometimes it's difficult to find things out when you're one in a group of 25/30. You often don't feel able to raise questions because they might seem silly when everyone else understands something.'

(Jaclyn)

'The teachers here are really good. They interact a lot with the pupils and get involved. If you need help with something they take time at lunch time or in the breaks to go over it with you. Many of them are involved with the orchestra and the band and choirs, so they're giving up their free time to help the pupils and give them something. I'm able to play the cornet and the saxophone; I'm in the orchestra and a swing band. It's all really good.'

(Victoria)

'I'd pay teachers more. To encourage the most able people into teaching you need to pay them well – otherwise they'll go off and do something else so that they can earn more money from it. It's a really difficult job. For my community service I worked with a Year 7 group at maths, and I found it incredibly difficult. If I explained it once and they didn't understand, I got very stuck as to how else to explain it to them and make them understand!'

(Clare)

'I think teaching is a hugely challenging job, because you have to take on all these people who most of the time don't want to listen: who just want to go home and do their own thing, and it's just not in their minds to do the work.'

(Peter)

'Good teachers get you interested in the subject. They talk to you and it's like having a conversation. It doesn't really feel like you have actually been in a lesson.'

(Andrew)

'They've got to be enthusiastic about what you do as well as what they're teaching. A good teacher marks you on a scale of one to ten and it changes with the effort you put into it. As you grow up the teacher has got to change with you. If he teaches a spectrum of classes from Year 7 to the sixth form, then he's got to change the way he teaches from lesson to lesson. There are people that will never get on with a certain subject and I think you've got to be sympathetic to that as well.'

(Joshua)

## On friendships . . .

'We cheer each other up. Sometimes we're sitting in the common room – and we're 18 but we look like 30-year-old women because we're so depressed. It's terrible. But the good thing is that one minute we can be like, "Oh God, we've got this to do, and that to do." Then we can pick ourselves up. We laugh. We know how to wind down and not get too frustrated.'

(Amel)

'Because we are all experiencing A levels at the same time, we can relate together more easily than with our parents. They don't understand how hard it is, but we're all at the same stage.'

(Manmit)

'The friends you make are so important. You're first struck by the difference between senior school and junior school. You go away and think, "Don't know anyone". A week later you've got a form full of friends. But you lose your friends when you change schools. There were five from my year who came to this school from primary school. Now Alison and I are the only two left.'

(Gareth)

'You're split up from the friends that you made in primary school and put with new people. That gives you a wider range of friends in the end, because you're meeting new people.'

(Simon)

'I've done a straight progression from feeder infant to feeder junior to feeder secondary, so I've had a close group of friends of my age. It's no longer exactly the same friends as I started off with, because a lot have gone to college, but there were five of us who were in the same class for 11 of the 13 years I've been in school, so I've always had a stable core group. In addition, because I've never been streamed or setted, I've had friends of different academic abilities and from a wide range of backgrounds.'

(Karim)

'I'd say being with friends is the most important thing. It makes it easier to learn and a lot more fun. Otherwise you're sitting on your own.'

(Nicola)

'Really, it's about being with friends. If you didn't come to school and went to work, it wouldn't be such fun. If you were at home you'd get bored. But with your friends you just enjoy their company really and you're doing your work as well. It's not as if you just sit here at your desk, taking in knowledge; you're being with your friends.'

(Nawaz)

'You wouldn't come to school if you didn't enjoy being with the people around you. You wouldn't just say, "Oh we've got to come here today to get education." You get up in the morning and think, "OK I can do a bit of work, and then there are break times and lunchtime when I can see the people I enjoy being with".'

(Andrew)

'If I had younger brothers or sisters starting at secondary school, I'd say it's going to be hard when they start making friends and going to new places. You've just got to try and communicate with other people and learn the way other people think. You don't have to go along with it if you don't agree with it, but you have to be open to other people's opinions and take them into account. But don't put yourself in a place that you are not going to feel comfortable – you have to feel comfortable.'

(Kirk)

**On single sex education . . .**

'We've been in a single sex school from Year 7 to Year 11, but now there are boys in the sixth form. I've studied this issue and I think single sex schools are better. Boys tend to take most of the attention off the teachers, and girls are left to fend for themselves to plod through the work. I've always been involved with a youth club so I associate with boys there. I don't need that distraction in school. Most of my friends went to mixed schools, but I think I'm the only one who stayed on into the sixth form. The rest have dropped out. Being in this school you knew what you could achieve. I think the trouble is that a lot of girls get interested in boys too early . . . but then every ill society has I blame on men, because I'm a feminist!'

(Jannine)

'I've heard people say that it's not healthy segregating boys from girls: that being with the opposite sex is an important preparation for being an adult. But you can associate with boys out of school time. I don't think it's really that much of a big deal having single sex schools. It's not been a problem for me, because a lot of my family's friends are boys, so I haven't missed out on contact with them. On the whole I prefer to be in a single sex school because there's a lack of distractions.

Some other girls here might not agree though, because of the way they change when they get into the sixth form. It's as though some of them have never seen a boy before!'

(Manmit)

'Being with boys isn't actually preparing you for an adult role. Your adult role doesn't involve mixing with boys. The important thing here is your development as an individual within the school. Your adult role is not going to be dominated by how you get on with men. It's not unhealthy to be in an all-girls school. It's not like the whole school's going to come out as lesbians.'

(Amel)

'Even though we've been in a school for girls, we are still going to have to adjust to getting on with other girls when we leave, because we've been with the same group of people here. Even with people of the same sex you have to adjust. I didn't think having boys here would be a distraction, but some people that we've known as relatively calm people changed personality when they got into the sixth form with boys around – "let's party!"'

(Keji)

'Being in a mixed secondary school is different because you get to know girls as good friends. Obviously you get to like girls outside school. But if you had a relationship with a girl in a mixed school and then you break up with her, it makes it very difficult. I wasn't too bothered about there being no girls here, because I'd been in a mixed school before. I was pretty sick and tired of having girls in my class. Anyway we're surrounded by girls' schools here. There are three of them just up the road. The only thing we miss I guess is that if you do a subject like English, it's always good to have an input from the opposite sex. I found that when you had just boys in the class it was a lot different. Because we're in an all-boys school and because of the stereotyped response that we get from people outside, it makes everyone in here more homophobic really.'

(Mike O.)

'When my mum told me, "It's just boys there", I said, "That's no problem." At the age of 9 it wasn't a problem. We got here and it was all right for the first few years. Then suddenly when you're about 15, you realize, "wait a minute . . . maybe we should have been better off the other way." Having gone through it, I think it's probably better in the long run, because if there were girls around you just wouldn't concentrate; you wouldn't get the work done . . . especially having applied to university and needing three As.'

(Nawaz)

'Girls or no girls doesn't make a difference to me. I wouldn't say that we are deprived individuals who don't know anything about girls. I'm sure we do. Just because we don't see girls at school doesn't mean we don't have a life outside school.'

(Alex M.)

'The way boys treat you in the presence of girls and the way boys treat you in the presence of just boys is different. Machismo comes when there are girls about, and they are always trying to put you down.'

(Joshua)

'You can have a separate work and social life if you come to a boys' school. If you are in a relationship with a girl in a mixed school you might get distracted from your work. Here you can get your work done during the week and you've got the weekends to see whoever you want. I went to an interview the other day and I was the only boy amongst 16 girls. At first it was a bit strange. But I'm able to treat girls as anyone else – they're just people. Obviously girlfriends are different.'

(Alex D.)

## On private schooling . . .

'I went to private school and it's a very good experience. I was 11 and the facilities were excellent. There were lots of opportunities, the classes were smaller and the teaching was more focused. I wasn't concentrating at primary school so it was really good for me, because it got me back on track. There were probably loads of children like me in primary school who were messing around in class and not paying attention and weren't up to the standard they should be in their work. If they'd all had the opportunity I'd had, maybe they'd be back on track as well.'

(Jennifer)

'I think that if you went to a private school, you would be put under more pressure. Specially by your parents who'd say, "We're paying for this." My parents have said to me, "If you come away saying you've tried your best then we're happy with that." I always thought that if you went to private school, although you'd tried your best, you'd be for it, if you hadn't come away with good grades.'

(Gareth)

'You can't buy a good brain. If you understand things, take things in and are willing to learn, you can do as well here as if you went to a private school. Say there were twins with the same brain. One could go to private school, and the other to a comprehensive school. They could do just as well. You learn the same things. Why pay to go to private school when you can do it all here?'

(Donna)

'People who go to private school are better prepared for university – it's another example of the well off getting even more well off.'

(Lizzie)

'I think we need to change things so that schools are more equal. At our school there are lots of intelligent people, but we haven't got the same opportunities as if you go to a private school. People want to go there because of the reputation it's got with exam results. But that doesn't necessarily mean the teaching's any better.'

(Gary)

'I knew I wouldn't be able to go to a school where you have to pay fees. I've really enjoyed being here, really enjoyed it, but I'm aware that the dice are loaded against me because of the name of the school. If two people go for a job, the one from the private school might have loads of good grades but be a really boring person, and the other person sitting next to them might have just as good grades and a brilliant personality as well. But because they go to a comprehensive school they'll give it to the person from the private school.'

(Judy)

'Because the private schools can hand-pick their students, they're bound to get better grades, and then get more funding. If I was David Blunkett I'd direct where the money is going, so that some schools get more than others. It isn't fair that some schools have fantastic facilities, like sports hall, swimming pools, tennis courts, masses of computers, whilst others have very little. The ones in our school aren't very good. Everyone's on the Net and many of our computers haven't even got a floppy disk.'

(Jonathan)

'I'd like to change things so that how rich you are doesn't affect the level of education or the resources that you have at school. There's a private school near here and it's very expensive and there's a view that it must be a better education. But you need to ask, "Why is a private school any better?" Should someone have the right to better resources just because they're rich? I think we shouldn't have such a division in our school system. You either have one school for everybody, or you give everybody an equal opportunity to go to different sorts of schools.'

(Katy)

'Somebody that works as a managing director of a company can afford to send their children to private schools, but people who've really slogged their guts out in a factory or down a coal mine for the same amount of time and probably worked harder, haven't got the same opportunities for their children, even though they care about them just as much. The trouble is that you can't deny people the choice to send their children to private schools, but on the other hand you shouldn't deny other people the opportunity to go there too. There's a massive conflict here. If I was Secretary of State I'd force them to share with the state system.'

(Mike C.)

'I wouldn't go to a private school, because I think comprehensive schools give you something that private schools can't – a blend of people, a melting pot of experiences. You learn that what matters is you as an individual, not who your daddy or mummy are. I think somehow governments need to spend more money on schools through increased taxes. The problem is that if you're the party in opposition and you say you're going to raise taxes, then a lot of people won't vote for you.'

(Leon)

'If people actually knew that the increased taxes were going into improving education, then people wouldn't be so worried about paying more. My mum pays a lot of tax, but I come to a school where I have to pay for my books, my paper and for a lot of the materials I use, so she's paying for something that I don't receive. I know that in Scandinavian countries where they pay more taxes, they have much better education in general, so the need for private schools disappears, doesn't it?'

(Laura)

'I think there's a big problem of inequality between the middle classes and lower classes. Some children have a good education because their parents can afford to pay for it; they have good health care because their parents can afford it, and everything revolves around whether you have enough money to buy you these privileges. That sort of elitism is a real problem.'

(Natalie)

'Of course you can't stop parents wanting to give their children the best start in life. If they see that as an education costing a couple of grand a term, it's really up to them. In a democratic society you could say it's unfair to stop parents, who have worked hard all of their lives, choosing to spend money on what they want, even if that's an exclusive kind of education. The problem is though that such children are at a disadvantage. If they attend protected establishments, they are only mixing with children whose parents have the same attitudes and the same amount of money lining their pockets. They are hidden away, separated from the rest of a society that incorporates people from all walks of life.'

(Karen)

'If you've got a lot of money and you want to buy a BMW instead of a Ford Escort, that's an option that's available. If you've got the money and feel you should send your child to one of these schools then it's an option that's there for you.'

(Alex M.)

'My parents aren't very rich and they have only ever been on one holiday in their life. My dad works seven days a week and he says, "There's no way I'm going to let my children work seven days a week when they are grown up. I'd rather go through some hardship now, so that they can get a better job." We live in a house that's worth about £40,000, which isn't terribly much compared to people in this school. Everybody around us says, "Why are you sending them there?" and my parents say, "It's the best thing we can do for them." When I was younger I didn't like the idea of going to a school in a blazer every day, coming home and seeing all my friends looking at me. But now I'm glad I went to a private school. I know I've got a better start in life. I'm extremely grateful that my parents went through that sort of hardship. I don't feel guilty about it. I feel lucky.'

(Nawaz)

'The problem with phasing out the assisted places scheme is that those children whose parents aren't so well off can't have an equal chance. By doing that, we're saying, "OK, it's only the rich people who can go to a school like this." I wouldn't say that I'm particularly academically able. But because I've been pushed in an academic sense, it means that I hope to get the grades I need.'

(Joshua)

'You talked about trying to make ordinary schools better, but that might be a waste of money because a lot of people don't want to learn. I'm not saying, "Don't give them an education", but if you do want to bring up standards in education, you need to have a few schools that are better and people who want to go to them. Quite a few kids don't. They don't see education as a major thing in their lives. I think if you're willing to put the effort in you can do it in a comprehensive school, but often you don't realize that until you're a lot older. We've been made to put effort in since we were 11, so we're going to do well. A lot of kids get to 16 and then they suddenly realize, "Action!" In education it's just too late.'

(Nawaz)

# 5

# Looking forward: comments from sixth formers

**On what they'd like to change about school . . .**

'Every school I've been to the buildings have been falling to bits. You just accept it as you go along, but really it's not acceptable at all. I can remember the junior canteen having a leaking roof and water would drip down onto your dinner if it rained. When I think about it now, it's pretty disgusting, although at the time you just thought that you had to be careful!'

(Karim)

'I'd like to change the level of communication between teachers and pupils. You've got a huge hierarchy in school, with pupils at the bottom and teachers at the top. It's difficult to get through to the people above you.'

(Natalie)

'I think schools need to encourage and accept more independence. In one year's time I'll be going to university and whether I learn or not will be down to me. I'm not going to have someone standing over me all the time. Although there's more independence in the sixth form than when we were doing GCSEs, it's still not very much.'

(Nick)

'I think I'd make it compulsory for people to go to school till the age of 18. At 16 I feel people are too immature to make such important decisions. Many of them don't get a job, and that just leads to unemployment and more people dependent on the state. When I was 16 I had all sorts of funny notions in my head about what I was going to do. I wanted to be an anthropologist, although I hadn't a clue what it meant. They say, "Knowledge is power", but at 16 you don't know all there is to know. If you stay on you become more aware, more knowledgeable.'

(Jannine)

'Some of those who left at 16 still have the security of home, even though they're working. I don't think they've grown up in the sense that we have – doing A levels is a maturing process. I think a lot of people who didn't stay on missed out, not only on the academic front, but also on a personal level.'

(Amel)

'I'd have more drama in schools. In our English lessons we were made to do drama even if we didn't like it, and it helped the shy ones come out of themselves.'

(Gary)

'I'd put much more money into music in schools. Music seems to be overlooked as a worthwhile subject, yet it's so much part of our lives. I'd like to see that there's enough instruments for a whole class, so pupils didn't have to share. I'd also want to make sure that teachers didn't leave half way through a course.'

(David)

'There should be more focus on out-of-school activities for all subjects, not just the one or two groups that get to go on the field trips.'

(Manmit)

'You need to change the exam system. The general studies exam, for instance, is aimed at middle-class pupils. We looked over a paper a couple of months ago, and it's like, "Who was Beethoven?" Lots of questions like that. Totally alien. I'm not saying we're all thick, but we couldn't make sense of it.'

(Judy)

'I think there's a lot of wasted time and opportunity. Take PSHE (Personal, Social and Health Education) for instance. Much of it was just listening to our teacher who was no authority on many of the topics. We knew far more about drugs and smoking and drinking than she did. We all knew the dangers.'

(Karim)

'I'd want to see more done to tackle bullying. Some schools have anti-bullying policies, but I'm not sure they work very well. Getting the bully and the victim together in the same room can be really humiliating for the victim. I can't think of a foolproof anti-bullying policy, but I do think something should be done about it.'

(Tanya)

'I'd do away with uniform, not because I hated wearing it – I didn't run home and rip it off – it was just the amount of time teachers spent trying to enforce the school uniform that frustrated me. There seemed to be much more important things to worry about than arguments about the length of your tie, or whether your shirt was the regulation colour. I know they say it cuts down competition between pupils, but competition's there whatever you do. If it's not the uniform itself, it's the coat. If it's not the coat, it's the haircut, or what sort of computer you've got at home. Kids will compete in some way. I'm sure uniform makes teachers feel better, because it's a tangible example that you've managed to enforce discipline. If a new head teacher arrives at a school where all the kids are sloppily dressed, and he puts the iron fist down and makes them all wear blazers, it will probably get everyone marching in step for a while and have an effect in the short term, but it's not the be-all and end-all of education.'

(Karim)

'I'd change the rule system. Some rules are pointless, yet they lead to worse consequences than important rules. Wearing a coat in the corridor can mean a longer detention than you'd get for being late or fighting. Also in some classes you can get away with stuff and in others you can't, so it depends on the teacher.'

(David)

'I think you need to give pupils more free periods because you just don't seem to have time to go to the library, use the computers and things like that. For some of us that's the only chance we've got to use these facilities, and things just start to pile up at weekends.'

(Gary)

## On teachers . . .

'I would want to see more women teachers. In my secondary school all the important people were male. It was the women who would be the people who would talk to the girls about anything, but they weren't involved in the running of the school or the structure of the school. It was a very male kind of atmosphere around the school. I was there from nine o'clock till half past four and I was only really in contact with women for personal education and things like that. I'd have liked it if there were women in more powerful roles, involved in the running of the school.'

(Katherine)

'I'd like to see more young teachers. It's difficult to relate to teachers that are in their fifties; they've got different values, different attitudes.

With younger teachers they give you more responsibility for your own learning. The tables are more likely to be grouped together and you're expected to discuss things and think about things as a group, rather than have everything written on the board, copy it down, learn it, test next week. You've got to make the lessons enjoyable. Forcing people to learn lists and facts is not going to make education interesting.'

(Mark)

'I think we should have more teachers from ethnic minorities, because there's only one in our school. School's a socialization and is supposed to be a smaller example of the wider world. So people need to know that there are people from different cultures that have got professional jobs and got degrees.'

(Jannine)

'In every school at least more than one teacher needs to be able to educate children about the experiences of being part of another race or religion.'

(Manmit)

**On time for reflection and discussion . . .**

'I'd like to see more time for discussions. It's no good just copying things down from the board. If you can take part in a discussion it's an experience through which you can learn. If you've got a teacher you can look up to and respect, you're actually going to listen to what they've got to say.'

(Simon)

'When it comes to discussions and someone else has a different point of view, you stop and think about their point of view, and you can then take your point of view together with their point of view. You begin to realize that there's different points of view and you start to accept other people's positions.'

(Jennifer)

'I've got a friend who's had to cope with a lot of racism and prejudice on no basis except for the colour of her skin. It's mostly white middle-class students in this college and many of them think that this sort of thing doesn't really matter. But when you're the person on the receiving end, it does matter.'

(Katherine)

'A lot of people who are prejudiced never come into contact with the people that they're prejudiced against. I'd like to mix people together in schools, so that you'd have a range of people from different ethnic backgrounds, in a way that feels quite normal. That way you'd start to break down prejudice.'

(Tanya)

'In every school there are divisions between pupils. People have their own clique of friends. But I think you need to meet different people within a school and meet different opinions and different ideas. People are afraid to communicate with each other, and that needs to be changed. It's a hard situation to try to overcome, because you don't want to get a group together and then make them feel insecure because they don't communicate with each other. You need to make it a gradual process. I'd like to see us do more about the school environment and the way we dispose of rubbish. If we have to live in the school, it has to create a good atmosphere in which to learn. We have some recycling facilities, but pupils are not driven to use them. It's one thing telling people to do it, but it's better if you can gradually bring people up in such a way that they want to do it. Each individual has to feel that it's the right way forward. It's a different way of thinking.'

(Kirk)

## On ability, achievement and assessment . . .

'I was reading an article in the *TES* this morning, which was suggesting that more able children actually achieve better in mixed ability groups. I think it depends on the subject. With a subject like maths it might be easier to have a mixed ability group, because you can have children working on their own or in groups at different levels within the same topic. There are hard questions and easier questions, but they are on the same topic at the same time. It's possible for the people who are more intelligent or more motivated to do more. However, if the subject involves whole-class teaching, like English literature, that's much harder with a mixed ability class, because it's difficult to talk to all the levels of ability in the class. I remember in Year 9 we had to do books that were simple enough for people right at the bottom of the class to understand, so I found the books we studied, except for Shakespeare, quite boring.'

(Clare)

'I'd get rid of sets which divide people according to ability. I was in the bottom science set through my entire school life and we were treated like we couldn't do it, and we weren't going to get high grades, so we thought, "OK, who cares, we won't do our work." In English, though, we were in mixed ability groups, and that enhanced your ability, so my grades were higher in mixed ability classes than when I was with those of the same ability.'

(Katy)

'You can help each other if you've got different talents in a class. Someone who is really arty can influence other people, and that will happen a lot if you've got people who are good at a range of different things. If you're doing an essay together with a friend, you'll give them ideas and they'll give you ideas. It works both ways.'

(Jody)

'I think that sometimes it is necessary to split up people of different abilities. Everyone has different gifts. Some people are gifted academically; others gifted musically, or gifted as organizers as opposed to English essay writers. I think you're going to educate people more effectively if you split up different levels of intelligence. Otherwise it slows down the teacher, because you have to go at the speed of the slowest person, as opposed to going at the speed of the middle level of intelligence.'

(Matthew)

'I think it's important for schools to separate out those who want to learn from those who don't want to learn. That's not the same thing as having groups for those who are clever and those who aren't. But some pupils just want to muck about and that gets in the way of what almost everyone else wants to do, because the teacher then has to spend so much time sorting them out. The sad thing is that there are some pupils who don't see any value in being at school, and somehow we need to change that kind of attitude, because everyone must have things that they're good at, even if they're not brilliant at some subjects.'

(Lisa)

'Brighter children pick up ideas faster. So it's more efficient to separate people into small groups. A certain amount of segregation is a good thing, say for people who are extremely good at maths or whatever.'

(Andrew)

'In my primary school we had people in the class who were extremely clever and all the people in the class knew they were clever. But because they were so intelligent at maths they got very bored and they were getting into trouble. We knew that they were clever but the teachers didn't understand that. I'd say that comprehensive schools are not challenging enough. You can't make it too challenging obviously. But for a certain spectrum of the class it's got to be suitably challenging. Otherwise people are just going to coast. Also you're more likely to be victimized and singled out if you do extremely well.'

(Alex D.)

'If you're not good academically you're seen as a failure, but it shouldn't be like that. The fact that A level league tables don't include GNVQs and NVQs means that society doesn't really regard vocational qualifications as very important. There's different sorts of intelligences though; there's being intelligent by school standards and there's natural intelligence. Common sense is something else as well.'

(Nick)

'I think more needs to be done about making all pupils feel comfortable. The academic structure is OK, and people who do well from the top classes are rewarded at prize giving, but there are other classes who are not being given awards, not being told, "You've done this. You've achieved that." They're not being given the support to really experience a sense of success. Often it's only the elite who are awarded prizes and that creates a division between pupils. People may not be achieving at the same level, but they are achieving success nevertheless. Some of my friends are in these classes and they feel let down by the system.'

(Kirk)

'I have a part-time job at W.H. Smith's and I work in the book department. It scares me to see that we're selling revision guides for Key Stage 1. It just seems ridiculous to be pressurizing children into revision at the age of 7. This pressure may even put some children off. I don't quite see how these National Tests actually help the child; it's just an easy way to get statistics for comparison.'

(Mark)

## On the potential of ICT . . .

'The other day I was watching a video about physics and it had really tough algebraic equations in it. They used a computer to illustrate how to tackle differentiation. It was quite clear what was going on and I was thinking, "Well, this is probably the future." If you don't understand steps in maths or physics you can just click on a button and it will give you more steps and expand what's going on. You can use the computer to go into as much detail as you want. Also, with computers, people can see what is going on in the world over the Internet, and they will want to experience more of that in the future.'

(Peter)

'I'd give a computer to every household in the country. Or possibly use the two way digital system. There's so many possibilities for educating people through television, telephone lines and over the Internet. We already have the Learning Zone on the BBC, and The Open University has used television for years. In Sweden and Canada, where it's very difficult to bring children together in some districts, they do a lot of work using telephone lines and cameras. Alternatively, everyone could have a laptop and you'd carry it around instead of a bag full of workbooks, with teachers using electronic blackboards, where they can send messages to you. There would be a facility for students to hook up to the network in each classroom. The teacher can then send documents, take a register, show presentations, and read students' work from a main computer. Students' screens could also be available to view so as to ensure that they are working: an alert could be programmed into the machines to detect if anyone was playing a game! The teacher could download completed homework and send new homework to students instantly. This would reduce paper costs dramatically.'

(Matthew)

'The way the world is advancing technologically, the school will need to have a lot more computers around the building. The need for Internet access will have risen substantially, as every teacher and pupil will need help with their subject. IT and music will become much more prominent subjects than they are now.'

(David)

'That kind of scenario seems very artificial. I like the traditional method of learning. I'd rather that the teacher was there in person, than a computer. I wouldn't really want to ask a computer questions relating to my theatre studies.'

(Jody)

'There's a human element in learning that's important. Computers don't have the same body language and facial expression that you get from a person. It's just a screen. I learn things better by somebody explaining it to me, not by reading an explanation. The idea that everyone will have a laptop, and access to any kind of information they want through the Internet, will certainly give people access to much more knowledge. But a computer can't capture your imagination as much as a person can.'

(Clare)

'You can't be taught from the Internet. You only get information, not anything that tells you how to use that information. People can't teach themselves at home. You need someone to go over things with you.'

(Karen)

'Although the focus is on the new technology, there's not enough thinking about how to apply these new resources. It's one thing to have the equipment and access to email and the Internet. It's another to use it creatively.'

(Kirk)

'The idea that you could learn at home, without coming to school, wouldn't work. Computers wouldn't keep you entertained enough to actually learn everything you need to learn. You'd just end up doing something else at home. I think you need someone else. The subjects I like are the ones where I like the teachers. I'm doing maths A level because I had such a good time in the first five years of maths at school. I realize it's a really bad way to choose, but I know that's the way it happened. Teachers have to be enthusiastic and to motivate the class. That's what makes it enjoyable and makes you want to do it. A lot of people get into a situation where you just can't see what's going on – perhaps you've done badly in a test or something – and suddenly you start to hate the subject. It's just psychological a lot of the time. But as long as you can go back to the teacher and ask them what's going on and sort it out, it can become brilliant again. You think, "Wow, this is great, I can do it!" It's all about teachers making sure that you're OK. A computer could never do that.'

(Peter)

### On plans for what to do after the sixth form . . .

'I'm going to university to do psychology and then I'll work with special needs children. I've been involved with schemes where children come for the day during holidays to give their parents some respite. It was just feeding them, changing them, playing with them. I got a lot of satisfaction from doing that. I like the challenge of working with disabled children. There's some disgusting bits, some very unpleasant bits, and I've been quite upset by some of the things I've seen and had to do, but it's all worth it when you see a child smile. Some of my friends have tried it but they don't usually last an hour. Partly it's because they can't handle what they see and partly it's too much like hard work. It upsets them too much, which I can quite understand, but I really enjoy the work myself. The children are an inspiration to me and I can see something incredible in all of them.'

(Katherine)

'It might sound a bit pretentious but I want to go into the Foreign Office. So I'm going to study social policy at university.'

(Jaclyn)

'I'm planning to go to the University of Geneva or Zurich, because the economy there's much better. I'm going to take a course in French and German and Italian, and all my jobs are going to start at £100,000 a year. I'm not accepting anything less. Basically you go to work to earn money. Let's face it, there's nothing else . . . not really.'

(Jonathan)

'I always wanted to do teaching but I can't decide between studying English and history or doing a law degree. I applied to do both and I've got all my offers, so now I've just got to decide what to do. Everyone is saying to me, "Don't go into teaching, Amel; the salary's not very good." And I know that I could be earning £40,000 as a lawyer by the time I'm 25!'

(Amel)

'I'm doing my highers in maths, English, chemistry, biology and physics and I want to pursue a career in pharmacy when I leave. I'd also like to have done higher music before I finish here, as there's so much opportunity for studying it and being involved in the orchestra and various bands. It's brilliant!'

(Lisa)

'I see education as an investment. It's something you're building up. The higher you go in education, the higher the level of responsibility and salary it will put you on when you get a job. I think I'll just go straight through education. I know some people take a year out for work experience, but quite a lot just spend the time doing nothing and messing around.'

(Matthew)

'I think it depends on the sort of person you are. It certainly gives you a chance to decide whether you really do want to go to university. My brother won a scholarship to go to Japan for a year having got three As at A level. Now he's at university doing third year work because he's studying Japanese.'

(Jody)

'I don't want to go to university. My sister is doing English at Lancaster University. She's in the second year and she's already £4000 in debt. She's worked out that by the time she finishes she'll be £8000 in debt. I don't relish the thought of being that much in debt at the age of 20 or 21. You're going to come out with a degree but even that doesn't secure a job these days. Of course I'd like to get a degree, further qualifications and everything. Most people would choose to have better qualifications. But I'd be dependent on my mum and dad and that's not what I want to do. I've got a younger sister and they need to support her, so I don't want to feel I'm putting them under a lot of pressure. The way I see it is that it's the well-off people who get the better opportunities and a better education.

I'm a bit worried about getting a job, but I know myself and I know I'll succeed.'

(Simon)

'I want to be a primary school teacher. I've always wanted to help kids get a better education, and I seem to create a good bond with children. But I do worry about getting into debt. My mum and dad have been saving for me and my brothers to go to university, but getting into debt is still at the back of my mind. Even though Mum and Dad say they'll pay, it's awkward taking money from your parents. It doesn't seem fair that it's the well-off people that can actually go to university and get a degree – and then get a good job at the end of it and still be well-off. Some people say I must be mad to think about becoming a teacher, but I just say, "It's what I want to do." Money isn't the main thing in life, because as long as you're earning and able to maintain a good life, you don't need lots and lots of money to be rich. It's more important to do something that you really enjoy doing.'

(Alison)

'Tuition fees haven't deterred me. Before they introduced them I was certain I was going to university. Now I'm still sure. I appreciate that university education needs to be properly funded if we want a first-class education, and that the government doesn't have enough money. But it's hard for some people, because they know their parents can't really afford to pay.'

(Keji)

'I'm going to be a midwife. My personal view is that money is not the greatest thing in the world. Working with people providing a caring service, that's what's important to me. I don't want to go out and earn millions. I always think there are people out there who are worse off than me – people with disabilities, people homeless and people out of work – so I can't grumble. And we're nearly all rich in Britain compared with some other countries.'

(Donna)

'I want to do chemistry at university and then go into chemical research.'

(Mike O.)

'My ambition is to be a doctor. In my dreams I see myself as a successful surgeon.'

(Alex M.)

'I want to go to university and then make computer games. I'm going to have my own games company, but I don't want to be someone who rushes round in a sports car all day and just turns up for an hour. I'd still do work. I don't want to become someone who just turns up for their pay cheque.'

(Nawaz)

'Music teaching in this school has inspired me to want to pursue a 'pop' career. Watch out for the headlines in a few years' time!'

(David)

## On what they'd like to change in society . . .

'In an ideal world I'd make university education free again, because I think it's really difficult for working-class kids to go to university as it's so expensive. Some people say that if you make it free, then students will just mess round and not take it seriously, but not everyone has that attitude. There's people who really do want to be educated, but they just can't afford it, and they're missing out on the chance to get a degree and a decent job. That's not fair.'

(Jody)

'I would spend more money on education. When you talk to teachers here they tell us that they've got 3p per student to spend on us, or something like that. How are we meant to get a decent education and good results when they've got so little money to spend on us? I think the government has made a mistake in getting rid of the grant system. In a few years' time we're going to be the people that matter, so they should be looking out for people of our age. When they're only funding a select few, it's neglecting the majority of the people really.'

(Gareth)

'We need to increase taxation so that all schools can have good resources. That way it won't just be money buying privilege.'

(Karen)

'I would use more of the lottery money to spend on hospitals and schools, and hostels for the homeless, instead of theatre and the arts. I'd cut the money paid to some people for the jobs they do, so that there's more to share around.'

(Alison)

'If you compare our situation to countries who have got very little, you realize how thankful you should be that we've only got a problem with lack of paintbrushes.'

(Natalie)

'I'd do away with league tables. What they care about is not whether people have done the best they can, but how schools are compared with other schools. Results get published in the papers round here and one school I used to go to was proud of the fact that it got more than 50 per cent, but it shouldn't be like that. It should be proud of the fact that every single pupil has done the best they can, not whether the top sets achieve their As or their A*s.'

(Leon)

'The competition should be within the school not between schools, because otherwise schools concentrate on those who will get them points in the tables. They'll put loads of effort into those kids who are borderline C–D to bump them up to a C, but the kids who are going to get Es or Ds, they're definitely out. The trouble is that schools want you to give the answers that have already been given; they don't want you to think of an answer which, although not revolutionary, might be a bit different or a bit new.'

(Nick)

'I'm troubled by the focus in schools on league tables. In their need to be high up in the tables, they will concentrate on the clever ones and ignore the less capable students. Two of my friends were accepted into highly prestigious universities and the school was delighted and made quite a fuss of them; but it made the rest of us who were applying to other universities feel that we weren't as important.'

(Keji)

'I'd like to change our attitudes towards disabled people and the lack of facilities for them. I think it's a crime to do that to people.'

(Mike C.)

'I'd like to change the intolerance that's around. A lot of people our age are very intolerant of minority groups, especially black people and homosexuals. It really is horrendous. When I hear people say these things I think, "Am I the same age as these people?" They sound like 60-year-olds who haven't had to deal with anything. It's difficult because if you've got these prejudices at our age, they're going to carry on with you. I think prejudice is worse among men. Whilst women tend to discuss these sort of issues more frequently, men tend to avoid issues they feel uncomfortable talking about or discussing. Women can have their views modified by listening to the opinions of others, but men maintain a single point of view throughout life.'

(Mark)

'The only way you lose your prejudices as you're growing up is to experience situations where you're forced to find things out for yourself and you begin to realize that being different isn't necessarily a crime. In an ideal world you'd send 16- to 19-year-olds to a homeless mission once a week – maybe on their own so they can't find protection in friendship groups – so they have to work things out for themselves. If you're with mates you're up to taking the piss out of people, you know, jollying each other along, but if you're on your own, maybe . . . ? But I realize it isn't necessarily the job of schools and colleges to educate people in all aspects of life. Issues of racism, sexism, prejudice and ignorance have to be examined, but maybe it's your life experience that should teach about these, not the National Curriculum.'

(Jaclyn)

'Following the findings of the Stephen Lawrence inquiry I recently read an article about how British schools have been pronounced as racist. I don't know to what extent this is really true, as I've not experienced racism in either my primary or my secondary school. However I have experienced racism outside of school. I was saddened at the length of time it took for the Stephen Lawrence affair to be brought to main-stream attention, and I think it will be a long time before the UK defeats racism. I am sometimes angry when I hear people deny that racism exists. It is this sort of denial that allows it to continue. Educa-tion has a big part to play here, since attitudes instilled at a young age remain for life. Schools can help filter out racism.'

(Keji)

'I think young people need more representation. They need to be taken more seriously. MPs make decisions about things that really aren't going to affect them by the time they come into effect. It's going to be our generation that experiences the consequences. We are going to in-herit a lot of issues, such as Northern Ireland, the Euro, the monarchy, and we should have an opportunity to make our opinions heard. I'm involved in the Youth Council in York, and we discuss issues that affect young people, mainly leisure issues. Because York is a tourist centre, everything revolves around tourism, but we need to look at the leisure facilities for young people as well.'

(Tanya)

'Young people have this view of older people that they dictate every-thing, but older people know more because they have more experience. Everyone has been young and the issues for young people don't change, so older people can make sensible decisions about things that affect us.'

(Matthew)

'I'd do something about homeless people. There are loads of them in this city.'

(Ian)

'I'd want to do something about unemployment and homelessness. Having a job solves a lot of problems.'

(Donna)

'I'd like to get rid of the vicious cycle of homelessness. You can't get a job if you don't have a home, and you can't get a home if you don't have a job.'

(Mike O.)

'I think communism is a good idea. It doesn't work in practice but it's a good idea on paper. At least it would mean that the people at the bottom of society wouldn't be so low. You wouldn't have so many people so far above or so far below. You wouldn't get graded. If I was repairing someone's computer and the guy next door was cleaning a window, you'd still be on the same level.'

(Nawaz)

'I'd like to do something about inherited privilege. I thought it was funny that the Queen had to sign the bill to remove hereditary peers, since she's the prime example of that kind of thing. It was a bit like a turkey saying, "Let's have Christmas!"'

(Jannine)

'I think society is getting worse. For instance a lot of the younger pupils in the school are far cheekier to the teachers than we would ever have been. They don't seem to have the total respect that we used to have and they don't care so much about getting their grades or staying on at school. The trouble is that job prospects aren't so good if you leave school early. There's a few jobs in shops and factories, but many more jobs require qualifications and degrees, so unless the level of people going to university goes up, it's going to cause problems. Of course there will always be a balance between those who want to leave school and those who want to go to university. But unless more decide to go on to university there'll be big problems.'

(Victoria)

'The government is always making highly publicized efforts to cut down on pollution, but I don't think they are really trying to do anything about it. Many of the companies responsible for this are multinationals who make a significant contribution to this country's GDP. Governments aren't going to get rid of them, are they? But they need to make it appear to the public like they're trying to do something.'

(Keji)

# 6

# Ways ahead: some visions considered

> 'I have been thinking about what our world would be like if there was no racism. I was watching the news about Stephen Lawrence. He was murdered by a group of young teenagers in a racist attack. He was not doing any harm to any of the boys that night. I asked myself how and why this happened. I thought about my friends. I am black and I have black friends and white friends. We are all children . . . we are all human beings. My hope is that in the new millennium people will learn to live together, no matter what colour they are. Everybody is special, and if we all learn to love and respect each other, our worlds will be a special place.'
> Dominique Carter, age 9, in *Our World 2000* (Save the Children 1999)

The preceding chapters have offered a wide range of young people's views and opinions about different aspects of education in the UK. Much of it reflects an experience that has been generally rewarding, as we might expect from those committed to sixth form studies. This would support the Keele research findings of 1994, which affirmed that the majority of pupils are happy at school, with 90 per cent believing that their school work is important. Similar sorts of statistics were gathered by the National Foundation for Educational Research (NFER) in its own study prepared for the National Commission on Education (1993), which indicated that over 90 per cent of 14-year-old young people think school is worth doing, with 95 per cent believing that schools should teach things useful for jobs, and 97 per cent saying that their parents think it is important to do well in school.

Support for the notion of schooling is clearly running high. In the same breath, though, the National Commission observed that over half of 14-year-olds say that most of the time they don't want to go to school, with one in four admitting to playing truant and one in five denying being happy at school.

There seems to be something of a paradox here. Young people believe schooling is important, yet more than half say they don't want to go to school. They want schools to teach useful things, yet 60 per cent count the minutes to the end of their lessons. Ninety seven per cent say their parents think school is important, yet one in four admits to playing truant. Could it be that they appreciate the opportunities which schools provide for making and meeting friends, they recognize the importance of examination success and they acknowledge the value of staying on after the age of 16 but, at the same time, they want to see some significant changes in the structures, the processes and the content to make the day-to-day experience more exciting and meaningful?

Many of their remarks offer some constructive suggestions as to how things might be different, both in relation to schools and the world beyond the school gates. As well as arguing for changes that would affect their own circumstances, many of them voice concerns about inequalities and indicate ways these might be tackled. There are messages here that can certainly add to and influence our own thinking as adults with experience of life beyond school. As the twenty-first century gathers momentum and the millennium prayer becomes a fond memory, alongside the fireworks on the Eiffel Tower and the images in the Dome at midnight, perhaps we need to remind ourselves of the hopes and aspirations we shared and aired on 1 January 2000 for making the world 'a better place'.

In the following chapters the comments of these young people are used as the basis for a dialogue with a number of adults involved in the analysis, formulation and implementation of policy and practice throughout the UK. Before doing this, though, it may be helpful to reflect on what some contemporary educational experts have written about possibilities for reshaping schools and restructuring the context in which they operate, and consider the extent to which recent government initiatives have started to address these issues.

In *The Mosaic of Learning: Schools and Teachers for the Next Century* (1994) David Hargreaves, then Professor of Education at Cambridge University, used the NFER survey findings for the National Commission on Education mentioned above to illustrate the extent to which the long tail of underachievement has to be tackled if Britain is to maintain (or regain?) its position as a world-class economy, able to sustain a high level of skilled employment. Alongside an enhanced role for interactive technologies and more reliance on high-quality research to inform policy decisions, he identified some structural changes that would help make schools 'sources of satisfaction to those who teach and learn'.

David Hargreaves advocated the separation out of administrative and management functions from academic and pedagogical functions within schools, so that the best teachers aren't sucked into senior management posts simply for reasons of career advancement. Brilliant classroom teachers don't necessarily make for effective head teachers. He proposed a much flatter professional hierarchy, and drew parallels with hospitals, so that teachers would have a comparable status to doctors and be supported by classroom assistants (as doctors are by nurses) who are able to supervise, manage and control children, leaving the design of the curriculum and the organization of teaching and learning to the specialists.

The government's attempts to restructure the pay and reward system for teachers could be seen as a move to implement one aspect of this, encouraging 'good' classroom teachers to stay in the classroom through enhanced salaries. Alongside this, an expansion of the training programmes for classroom assistants will allow teachers to concentrate more on the pedagogic function that currently only occupies them for a small amount of their day. If all secondary schools have access to learning mentors who will devote the majority of their time to those individuals who need extra support in order to realize their full potential, as is already happening through the Excellence in Cities programme (DfEE 1999), this will reinforce the notion of the teacher as specialist. Given that the young people interviewed here (like previous generations) say how much they value interaction with teachers, anything that 'frees up' staff to do this is clearly an investment worth making.

Recognizing the multicultural, multi-faith and multi-interest society in which we live, David Hargreaves also argued for diversity of provision of schooling, with an expansion of specialist schools such as we have seen in relation to science, technology, languages, arts and sports, and an expansion of diversification along philosophical, ideological or religious lines. There are parallels here with the leisure industry's array of holidays on offer. Whilst Benidorm and Ibiza may be heaven for some, they could represent hell on earth for those who would rather opt for the desolate wildness of the Scottish Highlands or the quietness of a Cotswold village. *Excellence in Cities* (DfEE 1999) spelt out the government's aims for designating 800 schools as specialist schools by 2003, as part of its commitment to raising achievement.

At the same time as advocating the above strategies, David Hargreaves stressed the need to establish 'a first and public language of citizenship', which would provide some social cement to bind together the different cultural, linguistic and religious groupings in the UK's schools. With an expansion of diverse schools, it becomes even more important that there is a framework in place for promoting a shared set of the values that are at the core of a civic, moral and religious education – whatever the faith. He criticized previous governments for mistakenly focusing on religious education as the basis for fostering moral development. The notion of citizenship that Hargreaves espouses is more than just an appreciation of civic virtues and an acceptance of decent social behaviour.

It should be a matter of deep concern that so many young people are politically illiterate, they have little understanding about quite basic political concepts such as democracy, and frequently display boredom, indifference or cynicism in relation to political issues and participation.

But how can there be any form of community participation that is not in some sense political? Community participation stripped of its political content is no more than self-serving neighbourliness. Active citizens are as political as they are moral; moral sensibility derives in part from political understanding; political apathy spawns moral apathy.

(Hargreaves 1994: 38)

This is precisely what many of the young people interviewed here would welcome and have welcomed: the opportunity to engage in real-life, community activities – be it mentoring Year 7 groups within their own school, supporting some charitable activity in the local elderly person's home, or engaging in some action whose purpose was to improve society in some way, such as working for Oxfam. The recommendations by Professor Bernard Crick's Committee on Citizenship (QCA 1998), with the emphasis on three 'strands' (social and moral responsibility, community involvement, and political literacy) provide a rationale for schools and teachers to take the lead in generating exciting opportunities for young people, building on the many local and national initiatives already in place (Brockington 2000).

In raising the profile of citizenship in schools there are some interesting parallels here with developments that have been part of the long-established traditions in Scandinavian countries for decades, and these are examined more closely in Chapters 13 and 14. Suffice it to say, at this point, that expansion of diversity of provision of schools can happen alongside celebration and maintenance of national identity, as long there is explicit and active commitment to a set of commonly shared values.

David Hargreaves's commitment to a 'shared set of the values that are at the core of a civic, moral and religious education' is a recurring theme in the writings of those who offer a vision of education in the future. In an article entitled 'Glimpse of Tomorrow', Peter Mortimore, director of the London Institute, ponders how schools might change in the next 100 years and envisions that the principal changes will concern attitudes to learning and promotion of achievement among *all* learners:

We need to incorporate the values and provide a school structure appropriate for future citizens of a modern democratic state. Thus, knowledge and its acquisition through learning, high levels of work related skills, good social skills, a collaborative attitude, enterprise and initiative, as well as the need for tolerance, perseverance and humour, should underpin any attempts at school re-structuring.

(1994: 13)

Around the same time, in an occasional paper for the Secondary Heads Association entitled *Tomorrow's School*, Anita Higham, principal of Banbury School, put 'values, boundaries and personal responsibility' at the heart of learning:

During my 35 years of working as a teacher in various roles, the biggest change is not the arrival of comprehensive schools, CSE, GCSE, the ever changing national curriculum . . . but the change of *values* in the young and in their parents: the verbal and physical violence to each other and especially to those in authority (which includes us as teachers), the awful bullying, the often awful levels of materialism and utter self interest, the horrendous experience of so-called family life and the consequences of its breakdown for nearly one third of our nation's student population; the insistence on 'me first and me last'.

(Higham 1995: 15)

Values are also important to Charles Handy, whose book *The Empty Raincoat: Making Sense of the Future* (1994) is much quoted by both Anita Higham and David Hargreaves. Charles Handy links values to the issue of national and regional fragmentation. In his first chapter, headed 'We Are Not Where We Hoped To Be', he considers the unrealized dreams and aspirations of the twentieth century:

Even if we ignore, for a moment, the turbulent conflicts in the old Russian empire, the endless dilemmas of the Middle East, the pitiless wars and famines of Africa and our continued inability to save what is left of the global environment for our grandchildren, there are enough problems in what we thought were the triumphant capitalist nations to make us wonder if we have missed the road to the future which we thought that we had won.

(Handy 1994: 13)

He looks at the progress of the years leading up to the end of the twentieth century and notes that despite our best intentions, while the rich have got richer, the poor have got poorer. In Handy's view we are on the 'edge of chaos' – the time of turbulence and creativity out of which a new order may jell, if we can learn to live with a number of paradoxes: such as the paradox of justice, where capitalism depends on the principle of inequality, which is only acceptable in a democracy if most people have an equal chance to aspire to that inequality. Or the paradox of intelligence, which becomes the new source of wealth for businesses and consequently a new form of property, yet it is impossible to leave it to your children when you die. Or the paradox of work and time with stressed-out executives working 70 hours a week and wanting to trade some of their salary in for time, while millions with time on their hands are seeking that elusive job.

He warns of the dangers of a divided society in which a third of the workforce are involved with routine work, such as packing airline meals and operating tills in supermarkets, with another third working as personal service providers in hospitals, restaurants and security firms, and the other third as 'knowledge workers' – the highly paid architects, lawyers, doctors, managers, financial analysts and such like, who use intelligence as the source of their power and are getting richer by the minute.

Although this huge inequality in income has long been justified on the grounds that wealth would 'trickle down' to the poorer groups through redistributive taxation, Handy challenges this assumption. If the most affluent members of society don't travel on public transport, or send their children to the local schools, or use the local hospitals or dental practices, or ever venture into the seamier parts of the towns and cities in which they live, why should they continue to pay for those things that are of no benefit to themselves?

It was a question Margaret Thatcher was able to use for electoral gain in decrying the 'nanny state' and encouraging individuals to look to the private sector for their health care, education, transport and telecommunication. Lowering taxes would free people to make their own choices about spending their own money. It allowed for government spending on some public services to be cut (in the interests of promoting efficiency gains) and others of these services to be sold off, with some disastrous consequences.

> As a result of a disgraceful failure to invest over a 20 year period, the quality of our school buildings is often shocking, even though many good schools work tremendously hard with what they've got. The excuse that times have been hard is certainly not acceptable. Those same 20 years have seen the sale of many publicly owned companies. As Harold Macmillan put it the family silver has been sold off. The most scandalous in a long line of such sales is the Railtrack flotation under which the entire rail network is being sold off for a mere £1.8 billion, just over one month's spending on schools.
>
> (Barber 1996)

The contrasting of the income from the Railtrack flotation with the expenditure required to bring schools up to standard seemed bitterly (if unknowingly) ironic in the wake of the Paddington rail disaster of October 1999, and subsequent reports that indicated Railtrack would like to sell itself back to the government to ensure that adequate funds were invested in safety provision (*The Guardian*, 23 October 1999).

Michael Barber wasn't entirely accurate, though. Capital investment hadn't been reduced in *all* schools. The City Technology Colleges and the grant maintained sector were in receipt of huge sums of public money for new buildings. In most of the areas in which CTCs were built there was absolutely no need for an additional school. There was plenty of surplus capacity in the LEA schools, which could have done tremendous things for their own buildings and pupils with the money that was invested in these dream palaces of science and technology.

> 'It was like a magnificent space ship had landed close by with the intention of sucking away our brightest pupils. All the staff were invited

to visit it just before it opened – a special preview of what was on offer. I felt physically sick to see it. We were numb for days afterwards as we looked at our own buildings and resources which seemed so utterly lousy in comparison. It was nearly the death knell of this school.'
(Teacher in an established comprehensive school
less than a mile from the new CTC)

The young people interviewed here would nod their heads in agreement. They speak of tatty buildings and describe toilets that no self-respecting person would venture into for anything more serious than a quick pee or a fag. Fortunately things are beginning to change. One of the first moves of the new Labour government in 1997 was to earmark £350 million for school buildings, and to allow local authorities to use proceeds from sales of other resources to supplement their maintenance and new works programme. In David Blunkett's words, the battered kettle and grimy chairs that have become symbolic of school staff rooms need to become a thing of the past.

Shortly before the Labour Party came to power in May 1997, Michael Barber, the critic of the Railtrack flotation quoted above, wrote *The Learning Game* (1997). As one of the people involved with the creation of Labour's education policy and now head of the Standards and Effectiveness Unit of the DfEE, he is responsible for policy implementation – attempting to make the vision a reality. It is interesting to examine the ideas in his book.

Like Charles Handy, Michael Barber highlights some of the paradoxes around us – the walk along the Strand late at night, past the Savoy Hotel and the Waldorf Hotel with their opulent elegance, while down the unlit streets, beside the hot air vents from both hotels, lie crumpled figures wrapped in an assortment of newspapers and cardboard boxes. Or the paradox of the fact that some of the poorest societies on earth possess large stocks of the most effective instruments for human destruction. Barber bequeaths to the next generation the task of bringing the juggernaut of 'unfettered materialism' under control, while managing the social consequences of doing so.

A well balanced thoughtful society would surely give the highest imaginable priority to ensuring that its young people were well prepared for this awesome destiny. It would examine the upbringing and education provided for its young and ask whether the arrangements were equal to the task . . . In choosing solutions, the need to take risks, to be radical and invest time, money and energy, even at the expense of present comfort would be recognised because everyone would be conscious that the risk of doing nothing would be infinitely greater.
(Barber 1997: 17)

Global responsiveness is a recurring theme for him (Barber 2000) and, interestingly, his own vision of how things might be in *The Learning Game* is prefaced by a quotation from *The Empty Raincoat* (1994). For Michael Barber, as with Charles Handy, the 'basics' for the twenty-first-century school curriculum require a commitment to the application of Howard Gardner's theory of multiple intelligences as a foundation stone for what follows. Gardner considers that we need a more humane concept of intelligence, which better describes the abilities, talents and skills that all human beings possess to different degrees. He explains how logical, spatial, linguistic, musical, kinesthetic, interpersonal and intrapersonal intelligences combine together to make up the unique individuals that we each are (Gardner 1983, 1994).

Because people differ in the strength of these intelligences and in the ways they use them, it requires a radical rethinking of how we teach and learn in schools, where the predominant focus is still very much on the logical and the linguistic. There is enough evidence, from research of experiments into accelerated learning, for us to know that a broader view of intelligence makes much sense. With this in place and a teaching profession that understands the implications for teaching and learning styles, Barber's 'basics' would then include a second language, transmission of the national culture, the ability to reason, heightened expectations of achievement, and a sense of moral community. On expectations of achievement he offers an interesting anecdote about a mother quizzing her son on his homework:

'Why stop there?' asks the parent of a 12-year-old boy.
'Because I'll get 10 out of 10. If I stopped sooner, I wouldn't.'
'But you've hardly spent any time on it. Why don't you go on?'
'Mum,' eyes raised fleetingly to heaven in irritation with this persistent adult. 'In our school, it's very hard to get more than 10 out of 10.'

We know of the Pygmalion effect – the power of adult expectations to influence achievement. Individual teachers can make a huge difference, as the young people interviewed in previous chapters testify. 'If you like the teacher, you want to work well for them,' says Paula.

Michael Barber argues for an 'individual learning promise', which requires a rethinking of where education takes place, a new role for schools, with a shorter formal day but a longer learning day, much more of a contract between parents, teachers and pupils, learning at home and guaranteed standards. Underpinning all this is a belief that the job of teaching needs to be taken more seriously, both by society and teachers themselves in recognizing their own learning needs and the enhanced professional status that can be accorded them if they allow that target setting and performance review have a part to play. Like David Hargreaves, he wants to see teachers supported by an army of classroom assistants, so that they can concentrate on the job of teaching.

In the book there are many references to Birmingham and Tim Brighouse, which is not surprising since Michael Barber worked closely with him for a number of years and was involved in developments such as the University of the First Age, conceived to raise aspirations and achievement levels of school children. He refers to Brighouse's vision and his capacity to enthuse the teaching profession.

> It seems to me there are three basic elements to teaching which are parts of what I call the 'golden cracker'. The first involves getting to know the child, the second involves the child practising skills, doing exercises, being occupied in consolidation of learning and the third is what I have called the alchemist's stone – the teacher's skill in intervening to stretch the pupil's learning. To mark the learner's mind we need to know its intricacies, its preferred learning styles, its different sorts of intelligence – motor, linguistic, spatial, musical, logical, scientific, personal. We need to know that the pupil's mind stands ready to do a deal with the other end – the teacher's extraordinary skill as an alchemist to the mind in transforming mental slavery to freedom. At this end lies the golden cusp of the teacher's skill: his or her ability to open the mind.
>
> (Brighouse 1994)

The 1998 winter edition of the *Education Review*, entitled 'School of the Future', took up many of the themes mentioned above, with Barber and Handy frequently quoted and David Hargreaves himself the author of the first article.

In his own contribution to this journal, entitled 'A wish list for the curriculum', Nick Tate, then chief executive of the Qualifications and Curriculum Authority, raises questions about the sort of society we want to live in as a precursor to examining how schools should respond. His own views are clear:

> We want a society clear about its fundamental values . . . one which celebrates humanitarians and philanthropists – not philanderers – on the front pages of its newspapers. In curriculum terms it means more explicit recognition of the more intangible aspects of human life . . . it means recognition that not everything that matters in education can and should be precisely measured. It means reward and celebration of these non-quantifiable and non-utilitarian achievements.
>
> (Tate 1998: 47)

Nick Tate's 'wish list' includes a strengthened role for the arts and humanities (recognizing their contribution to skills and qualities and a sense of individual and national identity), a shift in emphasis in science (to convey its essential excitement and its relevance, and how it involves moral issues), greater attention to practical skills (such as working as part of a team), a recognition of the role of ICT (without assuming it is the panacea for all our learning problems), and a prominent place to the study of religion and philosophy (something alien to the English school curriculum but not to the French). 'There is something rather splendid about a country which publishes the baccalaureate philosophy questions each year in its leading national newspaper' (Tate 1998: 48).

As well as the publication of *Curriculum 2000* by the Qualifications and Curriculum Authority, 1999 saw the publication of two interesting reports on curriculum matters. RSA's *Opening Minds* (Bayliss 1998, 1999) was the final report of its Redefining the Curriculum project and proposed a radical restructuring of education around a competence-led curriculum. Five overarching categories would provide the framework through which young people developed competences for Learning, Citizenship, Relating to People, Managing Situations, and Managing Information. The document provides some interesting examples of how this can be done through the subject framework, such as how the competence of 'managing risk and uncertainty' could be taught through history, geography, science, English and economics. This shift from information-led to competence-led is seen as the most effective strategy for enabling young people to meet the complex demands that will face them in the future.

*The Creative Age* by Tom Bentley and Kim Seltzer (1999a, 1999b), a Demos publication supported by QCA and the Design Council, examines how creativity can be woven into the curriculum. On the premise that 'creative skills – where the emphasis has shifted away from what we know and onto what we do with that knowledge – are the survival kit for the new knowledge economy for work and home life, and no pupil should leave school without it', they urge the government to reduce the national curriculum by half over the next decade, so that students can be provided with opportunities to transfer what they know across a wide range of settings.

In all these writings there are some common threads. They emphasize the need to establish more of a balance between knowledge and competences – towards knowing 'how' as well as knowing 'that', which is not to deny the importance of basic skills. Without a strong foundation in these, all else is useless; but we need to go much further and resource our education system so that it has the capacity to empower all young people. There is a need to examine the structure of schools and the way we organize the learning experience with regard to its location, its timescale, and its methods of assessment. We need to enhance further the professional role of teachers, by enabling them to concentrate on pedagogic rather than administrative functions. There is a need to grasp the opportunities offered by ICT, recognizing that they are tools not solutions. There is a need to clarify the values at the heart of education and ensure that these values are reflected by those in positions of authority. There is a need to confront inequality.

Inevitably there will be a reaction to some of these proposals. The Chief Inspector of Schools' view about what should be an appropriate model of schooling was expressed in characteristically provocative style in the first edition of the *Times Educational Supplement* this century, in which he lambasted the RSA report for its 'fatuous rhetoric'.

> The purpose of education in the twenty-first century is exactly what it was in the nineteenth and twentieth: to initiate the young into those aspects of our culture upon which their (and our) humanity depends. The national curriculum is a collection of academic subjects . . . and is an entitlement we must defend against the philistine enthusiasm of those who cannot distinguish between 'knowledge' and 'information' and who believe, in their utilitarian zeal, that the challenge is simply to define the competencies needed to manage our lives and work.
>
> (Woodhead 2000)

Predictably there was a flurry of responses to the *TES*, most of which challenged the point of view Chris Woodhead was purveying.

> Whose culture is Mr Woodhead referring to? The culture of the Surrey stockbroker belt? Or that of inner city Manchester? There is no such thing as a monolithic culture. To avoid an intelligent engagement with the realities of a multicultural society is very frightening in one so influential . . . Teachers deserve better advocacy than what you can offer.
>
> (Dr Christopher Turner, *TES* 14 January 2000)

> What rich irony in the criticism of those 'who believe in their utilitarian zeal that the challenge is simply to defend the competencies needed to manage our lives and work' . . . Would that be Ofsted's clipboard driven mantras?
>
> (Philip Delnon, *TES* 14 January 2000)

Given all that has been expressed so far in this book by the adults and young people, the Chief Inspector's remarks were rather disappointing, in that they seemed to focus on curriculum issues as if that is all that really matters in the contemporary educational debate. The only reference to values was a harking back to those of Victorian times.

Fortunately, there are others in the driving seat of educational reform who recognize that issues of inequality and access will not simply be resolved by curriculum tinkering. Some of these issues are already being addressed as part of government policy. Excellence in Schools (1997) has led to Sure Start (1999) and Excellence in Cities (1999) (see DfEE 1997, 1998, 1999a, 1999b). Reports and recommendations have been received from the various advisory groups on Citizenship (QCA 1998), Personal, Social and Health Education (DfEE 1999c), and Creative and Cultural Education (DfEE 1999e), together with recommendations from the Social Exclusion Unit (DfEE 1999d). The new century dawned with a great deal of activity in terms of government policy and practice. Tony Blair's millennial message insisted that education was 'a key economic and social imperative' and he committed the government to a 'fundamental modernisation of the comprehensive principle' (Sutcliffe 2000). A week later David Blunkett's North of England conference speech heralded even more ambitious plans to raise levels of achievement of *all* young people further (DfEE 2000).

Underpinning these statements and policies are some key values which define the thrust of the current administration.

> We cannot rely on a small elite, no matter how highly educated or highly paid. Instead we need the creativity, enterprise and scholarship of all our people.
>
> (David Blunkett, DfEE 1999e: 6)

> Our aim must be to create a nation where the creative talents of all the people are used to build a true enterprise economy for the twenty-first century – where we compete on brains, not brawn.
>
> (Tony Blair, DfEE 1999e: 6)

In addressing these aims the government have strong allies within the teaching profession. There are nearly half a million of them – most of whom are in teaching because they think they can make a difference.

> Teachers have a strong sense of values. They teach because they believe in something, and they want to see it conveyed. They have a conception of the 'good life' and the 'good citizen'. They know what kind of society they would like, what kind of personal and social values they wish to encourage, what knowledge they wish to convey and how. All these things are interconnected. Teaching is, at heart, a moral craft.
>
> (Woods 1995)

> We need to ask fundamental moral questions about what it is to live fully human lives and what is the connection between personal development and the wider social framework . . . and in the debate about such questions we must include teachers who mediate the inherited culture to the personal aspirations and needs of young people – who ensure that whatever the differences in cleverness and good fortune or background amongst these young people, their common humanity is recognized and their capacity to 'become human' is enhanced.
>
> (Pring 1995)

There are echoes of these sentiments in what the young people have said in the preceding chapters. They value the school as a social institution, as much as its capacity to provide them with knowledge and accreditation. What matters to them are friendships, the development of personal qualities, interactions with teachers, the environment in which they work, the resources available, and opportunities to explore, experience and contribute to the society of which they are part. Attention to the affective domain is high on their agenda. They want fairness and fair play and would like to see a society that reflects this vision.

In the chapters that follow these issues are further explored with some people who are very much involved with policy formulation and implementation of practice. The comments of the young people are used as a springboard for the interviews with David Blunkett, Tim Brighouse, Anita Higham, Richard Pring, Nick Tate and Ted Wragg. It is very interesting to see the values reflected in their individual journeys through the world of education and in their respective writings (e.g. Blunkett with MacCormick 1995; Higham 1995; Tate 1998; Brighouse 1999; Pring 2000; Wragg 2000).

# Interview with David Blunkett MP
## Secretary of State for Education and Employment

**Roger Crombie White**   Could we start with your own experiences of primary and secondary school? In your book you describe your very first day at Manchester Road School for the Blind with some evocative sentences that could well be used by teachers as a catalyst for creative writing.

> We alighted at a strange place, somewhere I had never been before, and walked up a driveway with the scent of newly mown grass in the air. I shivered as we entered the coolness of what then seemed to be an enormous building. A peck on the cheek, 'Good-bye son', and then they were gone. All I had ever known before was my home and garden, and a bit of the immediate neighbourhood. Now, for the first time, I was alone in alien surroundings, cast adrift, abandoned. The anguish I felt was heart-wrenching as I stood bewildered, fighting back the tears in the assembly hall. I was 4 years old.
>
> (Blunkett with MacCormick 1995)

**David Blunkett**   It must have been autumn. It had that quietness that Sunday tea-time has in a major city – well it used to have; things are slightly livelier these days! That stays with me, together with the loneliness of the fact that my mum and dad were going to leave me, and I knew I had to fend for myself. When you're 4 or 5 that's quite something.

**R.C.W.**   Many of the young people interviewed here describe how their own loneliness is assuaged through friendships.

**D.B.**   You make friends very quickly when you're at boarding school – you have to. However, since it's very much a collective, because you've been thrown together, the reverse then becomes true – that you cannot provide yourself with privacy. Because I had that all the way through to the end of my teens, I think it instilled in me as an adult a great wish and desire for privacy. Politics of course doesn't allow you a lot of privacy so I must be mad to have moved from a lack of privacy into a lack of privacy! But I still value what privacy I can retain. Our lives are full of contradictions!

**R.C.W.**   But you still manage to find some private moments?

**D.B.**   I do at home in Sheffield. I value those moments where you can just be yourself. You're not on show. You don't have to perform. You relate to friends as friends, and you are very lucky if you've got friends who don't let you down, especially in politics where people often think they've got friends, who then sell their story to the media. You can count yourself very lucky indeed where friendship allows you to be a natural person.

**R.C.W.**   After Manchester Road School you then went to secondary school.

**D.B.**   Yes, to Rowton Castle, to what has since become the Royal National College, a post-16 college rather than a secondary school. At the time, it took youngsters from the age of 12 upwards, who transferred to the senior part at 16 to undertake commercial courses – shorthand–typing, general studies, music and piano tuning. There was a rigid selection system at 12 for residential places at the two grammar schools, one for boys, one for girls, that existed at the time. I wasn't actually put in for the residential test because they thought I was too disruptive and wouldn't get through it. So I was automatically earmarked for the equivalent of the technical, secondary modern, which is what the Royal National College was then.

**R.C.W.**   Did you mind that?

**D.B.**   It didn't mean anything to me at the time. It didn't hurt me because I didn't go through something that I then failed. My big problem was that my father was killed just at the time when I was transferring from the primary to the secondary, which was a pretty traumatic experience. I arrived several weeks after term started because of my dad's illness and subsequent funeral. When you arrive late at a boarding school, everybody else has bagged your bed and wardrobe and made friends. So it was quite a difficult time.

**R.C.W.**   This issue of friendships has run through a lot of these interviews with young people. Some of them talk about how important it is to be with friends, and the way in which this enriches the experience in the classroom. Whilst others talk about how they missed being with their friends when they transferred from primary school and went in different directions.

**D.B.**   This happens, primarily, where there is some sort of selection. It's less true where there are equivalent admissions policies that ensure children generally do move up together and so retain their friendships from the feeder schools. Although, even in my own sons' experience, their friends did tend to go, at their parents' behest, to higher performing schools in preference. So you are right about that. However, they've managed to keep in touch with each other on a reasonably semi-social basis, and we need to look at the ways in which we can construct after-school activities – not just the study centres which we are already establishing, but broader educational, leisure and sporting activities to encourage and support the development of those friendships. Teachers can play a pivotal role here, if they can identify people of a similar interest, and encourage and support them.

**R.C.W.** However, even where they do transfer with friends, some of them talk about how they were then split up according to ability in terms of streaming and setting.

**D.B.** I notice that about streaming. It's less true of setting because you might be in the upper tier for maths but you could be in the same group for history, geography and English. Children have different teachers and move about a lot more in secondary school compared to primary school. However, where there's rigid streaming, people are inevitably thrown together according to the ability range that they have been put in.

I believe in setting though. I think that it's right – both for those who are struggling as well as those who are extremely gifted, because they can be given the help they need and people can develop their talent. It doesn't work where people can't move easily. My son was in the top stream for maths, but chose to move down a group very close to his GCSE final exam and did extremely well. Actually he did as well as anybody else, because none of the people who were in the top stream got more than a B either. It wasn't a problem for him, because he was making a judgement about what was right for him. I'm much more sceptical about streaming, because I think you end up presuming that young people who are good at maths and English are also good at everything else. This is the converse of what we are trying to do in Excellence in Cities, where the model we are putting forward provides individuals with the support they need for what they are good at, so that you can accelerate their progress. We need to look at how learning mentors, styles of teaching, out-of-school study and weekend back-up can all foster what young people are interested in, whatever that might be, rather than simply assuming they're either thick or bright as an overall assessment.

**R.C.W.** Some of those interviewed here talk about that – how they felt they were thick because they were placed in the bottom group.

**D.B.** The problem is that expectations and self-esteem go hand in hand, and both affect confidence. One of the things I learnt from my time at the Royal National College where we had quite close connections with Shrewsbury School was the extent to which overweening confidence was built in to individuals at the public school. They believed in themselves no matter how thick they were. We've got to develop that level of self-esteem, as well as self-appraisal, in all youngsters so that they have the confidence to build on those little nuggets that are inside every child. If they're allowed to flourish, instead of being suppressed, this will carry them through life. So the model of promoting the well-being of the individual and fostering that, in and out of school, is crucial.

**R.C.W.**    Yes, some of them talk about how they gain in confidence through involvement in extra-curricular activities, for instance.

**D.B.**    You can do that a lot. I see it with youngsters who have attention paid to them; which is the point of having learning mentors because teachers are very busy, almost learning managers now. If some of them can actually take on that pastoral role in terms of family links as well as an encouraging role, it could make all the difference. I know that in my own education a couple of teachers made all the difference. One was Wilf King at Rowton Castle who came down to college with me when I was doing evening classes. Another was Farukh Sharma, when I was going to Further Education College on day release, who just said, 'Why don't you go for university, why don't you go for it?' It made a big difference. Those little benchmarks in your life, those milestones, can really help. It's why we are interested in working with the Youth Support Service on the transitions between the teenager world and the adult world, so that there is a support system available, both in terms of advice and careers guidance as well as mentoring and back-up. It makes sense.

**R.C.W.**    Many of the students interviewed comment on the importance of conversation with teachers, and how they look to teachers for inspiration.

**D.B.**    And example. Schools that are doing well automatically have high expectations. They also have role models of ex-pupils as well as the expectations of teachers, so there is a roller coaster presumption of success. Whereas the reverse is true when things have been very downbeat and people aren't going anywhere, particularly in the eighties where the prospect of getting a job was very small and where others in the family weren't in work either. In some cases it's a generational issue. If we can break that cycle, so that there is a realistic expectation of being able to work and earn your own living, maybe it will transform their hope for the future as well. The New Deal is helping to do just this.

**R.C.W.**    Earlier you mentioned one of your sons. At the point where you came to choose schools for them, were you influenced by your own experience? Were you confident that the schools they were going to would give them the kind of things you would have wanted for yourself?

**D.B.**    I was relieved that the pastoral care of the school they were going to was renowned and was good. I was extremely worried about its academic performance, which was very low at the time and is still not phenomenally good. Therefore I had to weigh this very carefully. They did want to stay with their friends, they did want to stay in the neighbourhood. They presumed themselves that they were going to this particular school rather than across the city, which they could easily have done. Even at 16 – when they had the choice to go to one of the schools with sixth forms in the south west of the city – they still chose to go to the tertiary college. I put it to each of them that they had the option of going to one of the sixth forms, which have some very good A level courses. They were making choices with me holding the ring and being very cautious, because I didn't want to impose my own values. On the other hand, I felt a real obligation to work to make the system better, to be part of that process and to be a committed parent, which was what I tried to do. It's difficult to talk about this because I don't want to condemn parents who have taken a different view. Each of us make a judgement according to very different circumstances.

**R.C.W.** I appreciate that, and it leads me into the potentially contentious area of private schooling. You talk about feeling an obligation to make the system better and your own experience is one of supporting the comprehensives in Sheffield. Some of the young people interviewed here from state schools feel quite strongly about the issue of private schooling. There are two quotes in particular that spring to mind: 'If I was David Blunkett, I would direct where the money was going, so that some schools get more than others (in order to equalize level of resourcing in state schools)', and 'If I were Secretary of State, I'd force the private sector to share with the state system, because it's all very unfair.'

**D.B.** I don't disagree with either of those points. I think the question is, are we making any progress towards them and what are the constraints? Progress towards them is being made through the Excellence in Cities model. There are two policies that have not yet been criticized by any-body – Sure Start for the nurturing and development of parenting and early development skills, and Excellence in Cities. It is my intention to spread both as rapidly as possible. Excellence in Cities allows us to target resources, as do Education Action Zones to a limited degree, where we're putting in a million a year to some areas. However, the principal con-straint is that the general system of distributing resources is clumsy and we know that it needs to be revised. We have taken one step, which is to set up a Standards Fund, which means we can target resources much more directly towards key priority areas. We are able to do that with class sizes, with nursery facilities, and with numeracy and literacy strat-egies, based on need. We have not yet done it with the general distribution of revenue support and I accept entirely this is something we have got to get right to ensure that there is greater flexibility at a local level.

However, if we are going to keep people in the state sector, particu-larly in areas such as London and Bristol where there is greater seepage away from the state system into the private sector than any other major cities, such as Newcastle, Leeds or Sheffield, then we have to keep on board those whose propensity and income would be to go private. We have to stop people opting out by providing for them at the same time as investing heavily in those at the greatest disadvantage. The two issues aren't necessarily the same thing. It's to pick up Richard Titmuss's famous phrase that services which are only for the poor will inevitably be poor services, and to ensure that we engage the better-off in wanting to take the service up and then be part of the delivery of that service and its funding.

Given that we can't abolish private education, we have to try and work with it. We are beginning to engage the private sector in a real dialogue about how they can share their resources and expertise. Again it's this model of focusing on individual strengths, so that we can ensure that a youngster going to a state school, who requires additional support, can receive it, either virtually through technology on the Internet, or directly through additional classes.

**R.C.W.**  Tim Brighouse's virtual college?

**D.B.**  Exactly. The other part of the model is a straight, 'Well look, if you've got a particular talent and we can't meet it, let's meet it with the private sector.' The Wells Choir School would be an example of that, where there is real cooperation between it and the state sector now. We are putting some money in and Peter Lampl's Trust is putting money in. We are encouraging Peter to do this on a collaborative basis, because there is a tendency for the very rich to want to replicate the Assisted Places Scheme. We are saying we can help thousands of children if you work with us on joint projects between the private and the specialist schools model. Specialist schools can only receive money if a third of it goes into broader community activity and they cooperate with other neighbouring schools in sharing those resources. There has to be agreement from the neighbouring schools about which schools should get the specialism, so we've actually mutualized the specialist programme in a way that didn't exist before.

**R.C.W.**  You describe in your book the appalling circumstances of your father's death and your grandfather's death, and how these influenced your attitude to poverty and inequality. You talk about the constant struggle between those with power and wealth and those who have neither and you write about your determination to do something about this. What do you see as the most important things that you can do in the position you occupy?

**D.B.**  There are two or three key things. Firstly, we can actually create a literate and numerate nation. The foundation for further success in a knowledge economy has got to lie with people having those skills. The days of muddling through until you've got an apprenticeship in which you are then mentored by an older person, and you finally gain some sort of qualification, are nearly gone. So being literate and numerate; being able to gain the foundation to go through secondary education with some hope of coming out with something; freeing up the curriculum in the latter stages so that youngsters can experience the world of work and

engage in things that they are good at; creating a lifelong learning programme that really means what it says so that people can re-engage at
any time in their lives. All these are very close to my heart. But probably,
with regard to breaking generational disadvantage in the long term, the
most significant is the Sure Start programme which Tessa Jowell and I
devised before the general election. However, it will take fifteen or twenty
years before we fully know whether it will make a difference.

The other thing that will make a difference is introducing citizenship
and democracy into schools. First, understanding the world around you,
about what's happening and your part in it, and second, understanding
how democracy works or doesn't work. That involves appreciating the
constraints on governments and their power in terms of the modern
economy, and how you can therefore engage with the process. This
will actually stop there being haves and have-nots, in terms of those
who presume that they are engaged with decision making and those who
presume that nobody gives a sod about them so why should they engage
in decision making because nothing they do is going to change a thing.
I'm talking here about the way in which 'bread and circuses' really turns
off people from democracy.

**R.C.W.** Isn't the inevitable conclusion of that aspiration that some people
who have quite a lot will actually have to have a little less in order to
share the cake more equally?

**D.B.** Firstly, I don't think there is a finite cake and therefore we don't
have to take away to do it. What we have to do is to accelerate the access
to the bigger cake in a way that ensures that the gap between the haves
and the have-nots doesn't increase. Let me say two things about that. At
its very basic level the New Deal programmes for the unemployed are re-
engaging people. There can be no bigger have-nots in the working population than those who haven't had a job for six, twelve, eighteen months
or two years. The longer you are out, the more likely you are to stay out,
and the more likely, if you get a job, for it to be temporary and insecure.

The second concerns Information and Communication Technology.
Clinton made a recent speech in Florence about the haves and have-nots
and the dangers of this gulf. Tony Blair and I have been saying, for the
last two and a half years, that if we don't find a way of engaging those in
the most disadvantaged communities, schools and employment areas,
with access to technology and an understanding of how it works and
with an ability to use the information and the opportunity, then we are
facing catastrophe, because it will accelerate the gap and will reinforce
the dangers. So, that's why we are doing so much in schools with the
Grid for Learning, with the investment in training and its integration into
the curriculum, with the Loan and Lease schemes for parents to be able
to have materials at home, and with experiments that link homes to
schools, such as in one of the Education Action Zones. Learning centres

are now going across the country and, with the development of the university of industry, you can actually access these things whoever you are, wherever you are, in the same way that the library service created an opportunity for access so many years ago.

**R.C.W.**  One final question. You describe the effect on your own morale of your mother repeatedly saying to you, 'You're as good as anyone else.' Part of the problem for many young people is that they don't feel as good as others. All these resources that you describe are not by themselves going to do much about that, are they?

**D.B.**  Not unless people feel success at the end of their fingers, because success breeds success. The moment somebody finds they can do something well, they have achieved an attainable goal, they've met a target. A small example of this is children discovering that they can reach Level 4 in English. We are thinking through how we ensure kids who didn't achieve this, actually can, and what we need to do in the early stages of secondary schooling to ensure that they can reach the targets they've missed in primary school. We need to give people targets that are obtainable and workable, and then make that a stepping stone to something else so that it isn't seen as an end in itself. It's the beginning of the process of lifelong learning and achievement. If we can do that, then expectations will rise. I've had my own son say to me, 'I can't do it, I'm failing, I'm not up to this.' And I've replied, 'Well, let's work it through. Let's see whether you really aren't cut out for this or whether you can actually do it.' It's a question of rebuilding self-belief. We can do that in school and we can do it at home by working with parents. When I came into office parenting, family learning and what happens at home were not part of the Department's remit at all. We are just beginning to really engage with that – how we can work with the family to make them part of the solution. We need to help parents as well, so that their engagement will make it work for their children at the same time. The National Year for Reading helped a bit, as parents and grandparents started to realize that they were part of this process. We need rapidly to build on that, to make it work.

**R.C.W.**  Thank you very much indeed.

# 8

# Interview with Professor Tim Brighouse

Chief education officer, Birmingham LEA

**Roger Crombie White**   I'd like to start with your own educational experience of primary and secondary school . . .

**Tim Brighouse**   Primary school in Leicestershire. I went at the age of six, so I had less primary education than most people.

**R.C.W.**   This would be considered disastrous nowadays.

**T.B.**   Yes. I could read by the time I got there, unlike that lovely man, James Cornford, who went to Dartington. 'It was absolutely wonderful,' he said to me once. 'Mind you they never taught you anything. When I was nine, I still couldn't read. I thought you were only able to read when you wore glasses.' I like that story.

My school was a very small one in the next village. Lovely Welsh head teacher. Used to get biked there by my mum to start with, and I really enjoyed it, but very insecure. Took the 11-plus at 10, went to a direct grant grammar school in Leicestershire, and developed school phobia to the extent of being sick every morning and weeping before I went. Came back home, prayed I wouldn't wake up the next morning. Form order every week, loathed it. Never saw anybody smile. Full of dark shadows, absolutely awful.

Dad gets a job in East Anglia, move at half term. Go to the local, sleepy, country grammar school, never aiming to do anything except wait for what happens. Loved school from day one. Never looked back. Thought it was the most heavenly existence you could have. What an amazing, amazing experience that was! I suppose even at that early age I realized that schools could make one hell of a difference to your life.

**R.C.W.**   What was the difference?

**T.B.**   The atmosphere. Expectations were entirely focused on relationships and needs. You walked out into the playground and the teachers would pinch your crisps, they'd want a game of football, they'd have a chat with you on the way in, they'd have a chat with you at lunch time, they'd have a chat with you any time. They loved living there, they loved the school. The community loved the school. There was no academic pressure for achievement at all, but there was celebration of it when it happened.

**R.C.W.** Were you aware of secondary moderns around you?

**T.B.** Only when we started to play cricket or football against other schools, and I began to meet other children during the holidays. It was the fifties and I took part in debates about whether we should have comprehensives, and early on I remember thinking, 'Why doesn't everyone go to the same school?' Near my first grammar school there was a secondary modern school that had seemed in my mind like the salt mines of Siberia. I was wrong of course. The Leicestershire grammar school was the salt mines. At ten you can get these things wrong! Fortunately the East Anglian grammar school was not the salt mines; it was absolute, unalloyed joy.

**R.C.W.** And this was down to the atmosphere – you mentioned the teachers?

**T.B.** It had a tremendous amount to do with the teachers. Some were extremely good on the emotional intelligence and the commitment of walking that extra mile.

**R.C.W.** This is very interesting. Like yourself the young people interviewed here rate the quality of the teachers as important – that and their friendships. But some might say that the things they describe as significant, like your mention of nicking crisps, are almost trivial.

**T.B.** They're not. They *are* significant. I once followed a teacher around at a Cheshire school from the beginning of her day to the end of her day. I counted her conversations and interactions with kids, both in the classroom and in the bits before school, between lessons, at break and after school. And she had four hundred conversations outside of the lessons with different kids, if you count a conversation as something that provoked an exchange, whether the exchange was verbal or in acknowledgment of a glance or a grin or whatever. All of them were reinforcing, building, filling the cup full.

**R.C.W.** Where did you go from your East Anglian grammar school?

**T.B.** Oxford University. St Catherine's. I tried to get an open scholarship to Merton or Magdalen, but they rejected me. I remember sitting in these forbidding halls in Magdalen and Merton, which reminded me of being at my Leicestershire grammar school. I was surrounded by boys who seemed to have read everything under the sun, whereas all I'd read was the quotes from the books rather than the books themselves. But St Catherine's was run by Alan Bullock, who was working with Alec Clegg and forging a link between the West Riding and Oxford, so lots of northern grammar school boys were going to St Catherine's. It was for the kind of ne'er do wells like myself – the tinkers who came in by the wrong gate – and they let me in.

It was close to the police station, and we used to earn our beer money by going on identity parades. It was a good earner. The fortunate thing for us is that most crime is committed by young people, so university undergraduates, especially if they looked fairly straggly like me, were good for identity parades.

**R.C.W.** Didn't you worry you might be picked?

**T.B.** Occasionally I was, but I had faith in British justice; the police had got their suspects. If the identity parade didn't work, they'd try something else.

**R.C.W.** After grammar school and university you went into teaching. Why?

**T.B.** Because I'd been persuaded that grammar school was such a wonderful life. I liked the people there. I liked the world they had. I thought it would be a good world to be in.

I did a PGCE (Postgraduate Certificate in Education) and then I taught in a girls' grammar school and then in a secondary modern. In the girls' school I thought, 'You don't really need training to be a teacher.' In the secondary modern school it changed to, 'There's more to teaching than I first thought.' My ambition was to be head of a comprehensive school and I'd gone into this secondary modern school (which was also a community college) as deputy warden. The head there was slightly loony. He used to dash into the toilet to hide from angry parents and leave me to deal with them.

There was a job going in Sites and Buildings in the LEA. The head down the road said, 'Why don't you have a go for it?' I said, 'But I want to be a head.' And he said, 'You'd enjoy this – it's all to do with going comprehensive.' So that's how I went into administration. And I loved it really. I loved it because of what you could do. Nowadays, in local education authority administration, you've got a lot of responsibilities but you've not got much power. To have lots of responsibility and no power is really wonderful because you've got to influence people, and you will only survive by the force of your argument. If your argument is good enough, then people will listen. If you can persuade people in this way, you've actually got more chance of making any changes really stick.

**R.C.W.** There are echoes there with one of the things Richard Pring says about the time he worked for the Civil Service, where he had to learn to construct succinct arguments. I'm curious though. After your own quite privileged educational experience in a grammar school and then Oxford University, why did you want to work with comprehensive schools? Isn't that a bit like going back to the salt mines?

**T.B.** Don't forget we are talking about the end of the fifties, the beginning of the sixties. I'm a child of the generation that produced the 1944 Act. We wanted to build a better world and comprehensive education was the way we were going to do it. We were driven by a sense of social justice. It was – and still is – a matter of principle. Should you want for other people's kids what you want for your own kids? You must want that if you want a society based on equality. You might then ask me why should it be equal. Why indeed? In the end it's close to religion I suppose.

I was fortunate to be on the right side of the tracks as a result of environment, a combination of nurture and nature presumably, but there were dozens and dozens of people I was meeting, who had way in excess of the talent that I was blessed with, but were caught in the wrong set of circumstances. We must create the right circumstances to unlock that talent. Surely what we want is people to fulfil themselves and, in doing so, have a commitment to use that fulfilment for the benefit of others. That's what I'm driven by.

Therefore it's our job. Whether we are teachers or whether we are heads or whether we are administrators, we're unlocking people, we're unlocking talent. You can do it as a teacher; a head can do it around the teachers; and an LEA can help create the environment in which the odds are increased for talent to be unlocked.

**R.C.W.**   Do you feel that you are still on the right side of the track in the sense that the track is pointing in the direction that you want to go in?

**T.B.**   Yes I do. Strongly. There are moments when I get very irritated, but I think for the very first time we are in an age that is not shackled by thinking that you need millions of unskilled and semi-skilled people who will be obedient and accept the horror of an undignified job. That's nearly all gone. We are in an age of education, of learning, technology, creativity . . . and we've got a Prime Minister who actually says that and keeps saying it, so I assume he must mean it. Therefore there's a political will that there has never been before. We are no longer talking about 'rationing success'.

What an amazing opportunity we've got in this country. If you look more widely to our global responsibilities, you can start to feel uncomfortable, but if we can develop our talent with a sense of responsibility towards others, we are at the right place at the right time. Because of the Internet there is a certainty that English will dominate the economic fabric of the world, so the environment for us is very favourable.

We've got a government that is keen on education and we ought to be able to unlock as much talent as possible. Now I'm not saying that they haven't inherited sets of mistaken application of market principles to the provision of public services and competition against others rather than against yourself – issues which ought to dominate the discourse of education. I'm not saying they aren't making amazing mistakes. They are. And they've inherited lots of things that they seem unprepared to change as rapidly as they should. But the battle is beginning to be won. For instance, the Social Exclusion Unit's report on 16- to 18-year-olds not in education or employment is the most promising report I've read this year (DfEE 1999d).

**R.C.W.** Yes. Richard Pring shares your optimism when he says that it's the first time in history that a Prime Minister, a Secretary of State for Education and a Permanent Secretary are using the state system, or have used it with their own children.

**T.B.** I think that's a very good point. But then there are the casualties of the system like you encountered in *Tales out of School*. And they are the outcome of a double think. They are the outcome of Tony Blair sending his kids to the Oratory, and the head teacher of the Oratory saying to me, 'I can't run a successful school unless I have the right to choose the children.' I'd go along with that. I reckon I could run a successful school anywhere if I had the right to choose the children! And that's a huge flaw, which I don't think, deep down, is understood by Tony Blair. But we'll get there.

**R.C.W.** How can you be so optimistic when you observe many parents exercising their choice and removing their children from the state system or sending them out of town to the leafy suburbs? Some of the sixth formers interviewed here are very conscious of the inequality of resourcing between different schools.

**T.B.** The government has put some things in place through their code of practice on admissions and the setting up of an adjudicator. Things are beginning to happen in areas like Wandsworth for instance. So they are tackling the virus in the system. They realize that parental choice was always a false prospectus.

But we need to make our city schools more attractive. The first thing is to change our concept of secondary schools. We have to create collegiate secondary schools, which in this city would become part of the 'Birmingham Academy'. Children will belong to a wider community in which enrichment activities occur beyond the 38 weeks they currently spend in school, and beyond the school day itself. Children are only in school for nine minutes of every waking hour, so we need to look at the 51 minutes that they are in the home and the community.

The staff would belong to the Birmingham Academy and would have the advantage of belonging to a healthy, strong faculty that is organized across three or four sites in the city rather than experiencing the exhaustion that comes from belonging to a very small unit that is struggling.

I would also change the school year so that part of the timetable remained metronomic as it is now, with French followed by maths followed by science. But part will be non-metronomic, such as a day a week devoted to intensive, interest-led accelerated or consolidated learning around a particular topic.

**R.C.W.** How do you get sufficient teachers on board to cope with that?

**T.B.** Interestingly many want it anyway. Science teachers often say, 'Look, I need double periods, not single periods; ideally I'd like a whole afternoon.' Ask language teachers if they'd like a whole week on French, and they'll say 'Bloody marvellous! We'll all go flat out on the French. But of course, there are only three of us, you know. How about the rest of the staff?'

So you set up a collegiate school and you have the opportunity for that comfortable metronomic timetable for 37 weeks in the year, and you only try a few days. If it works and people say, 'We rather enjoyed that,' then go for 36, and then we'll have 35, and so on. Non-metronomic timetables have been run at places like Stantonbury and some of the CTCs with great success.

**R.C.W.**  How about those who say, 'What about the National Curriculum?'

**T.B.**  They are dead right. The National Curriculum is really, really important and you do need to fit it in. The problem with the metronomic timetable is that individual subjects need so many periods, until in the end there aren't enough periods in the week. So you need to say, 'Look, has anybody worked out how many hours in a year we need for this? Would it be different if we had an intensive week or an intensive day? You could have a whole chunk there, just at the cusp when you needed to consolidate the learning.' The core is fine, but it now needs to be expanded.

Take Year 8 where kids start to loiter. If you looked at the English, maths and science expectations, you could have a week intensively involving them in a design or technology project that had thought through not merely what you were doing in terms of the plan, design, build and evaluate, but also what was being consolidated in terms of language and development, with regard to Levels 5 and 6, or Levels 4 and 5 for different sets of kids. How are we developing their language, their understanding of maths and science concepts, while engaged on a design/technology project?

Now, this might be absolutely right for Year 8, but it might not be right for Year 9, because we have got proper tests coming up at the end of Year 9 to assess where we've got to. Of course, we might eventually get to the point where kids take exams at the point they're ready to take them, and fill their pockets with accredited success in Years 7, 8, 9 and 10. So when they come to Year 11 . . . they've done four of them before they even get there.

**R.C.W.**  So you'd take away age-related learning . . .

**T.B.**  One day, people will look back and say, 'It happened.' I'm all for it at the moment.

**R.C.W.**  What other ingredients would you add to this Academy?

**T.B.**  As well as curriculum changes, we need to change the nature of secondary schooling itself, to overcome some of the rigidity and attract back into education those young people who have been turned off by their experience. Why shouldn't we add a virtual college, for instance, to cope with these kids who are at the wrong end of the system, who've been counselled out of school, or been kicked out? If you take the ones who are wandering the streets and offer them individual tutoring with someone who can really make a rapport, who can guarantee a tutorial bonding. There are teachers like that: amazing, barmy people who can cope with these ne'er do wells. Say you had a virtual college, with a distinctive logo, and a guarantee of a full-time educational programme that was a mixture of appropriate schooling, work experience and community placement. Each kid has an email link through a personal laptop linked to the city learning centres, which will be ICT-rich and offering week and fortnight courses. The capacity of this virtual college to stitch together a set of experiences that is right for individual children is infinite, especially if you have tutors who can make the crucially important relationships.

**R.C.W.** Sound a bit like Illich . . .

**T.B.** Fine man, but not to be mentioned in polite company. Rather like Dewey.

**R.C.W.** But how would you actually persuade these children who've dropped out to have another go?

**T.B.** I'm encouraged by that lovely quote from Shakespeare, 'All they're good for is wine, women, and being rude to the ancientry.' We've got to stitch together a system that might make that *not* true for some of those for whom it is true. We've got to do it.

**R.C.W.** This all sounds great, but you will be operating these structures and these schools – the University of the First Age, Birmingham Academy and the virtual college – alongside a system that still supports parents in making choices to opt out and send their children to grammar schools or independent schools. How does this square with your belief in 'social justice'?

**T.B.** It doesn't. It will be difficult to stop most parents demonstrating a kind of double standard. However much they say they want for other people's children what they want for their own, they would actually do it the other way round.

**R.C.W.** Was that your own experience?

**T.B.** No it wasn't. The city we lived in when the children were at secondary school had a comprehensive system. We bought a house and the local school was the wrong side of the tracks. But I knew it was a very good school.

**R.C.W.** But weren't you disadvantaging your own children when you had the power to do something different in terms of securing them access to higher education?

**T.B.** No, I wasn't, but I know that's the public perception. You see I was the wrong side of the tracks myself in terms of grammar schools, because I'd had two experiences of different grammar schools and the one I enjoyed was a school that never sent anybody anywhere. Yet I enjoyed it.

There is something much more important than the school you go to. Your own kids are more affected by yourself as a parent. They're only in school for nine minutes of every waking hour, so if you've done your stuff right in childhood they're going to make the right sort of friendships. Academically mine did OK. One was offered a place at Cambridge (but went to London); the other went to Liverpool. Both of them came out with first-class honours degrees. Both of them have got a range of friends and understandings that I didn't have because they went to a comprehensive school. Both of them know that, and their own kids will go the local school where they live.

**R.C.W.**  You're very unusual though. In my own city, more than 20 per cent of children in primary schools transfer either to independent schools or out of the city, and from some primary schools it's more than 50 per cent. It's disparagingly referred to as the 'white flight'. You're optimistic that this prejudiced response to inner city schools can be changed?

**T.B.**  Yes I am, and it will. The government is wrestling with it in terms of the code of practice and criteria for admission. They've introduced Excellence in Cities. The tide will start to turn in the other direction. There's a similar flight out of Birmingham, but I've now got posters in every primary school. 'Are you choosing a Birmingham school? If so, you are part of excellence in this city.' What does that mean? It means a talented and gifted programme. Extra resources' learning with mentors, the University of the First Age, curriculum enrichment, city learning centres. Stick with us if you want your children to enjoy this. We think they will.

**R.C.W.**  Do you highlight the quality of teaching? These young people are clear about the importance of good teachers.

**T.B.**  Yes, of course. We've got the best teachers, best leadership, and best sports service. Children in Birmingham schools are lucky. Pity for the rest but it's just one of those things. We attract the best student teachers as well. Last week I was talking to one who'd moved here from London. 'Why did you apply here?' I asked. 'I want to be in Birmingham; it's where it's at. The future lies here.' Tremendous, isn't it?

**R.C.W.**  Richard Pring mentioned the problem of some of his best students going off to the independent sector because they get offered packages that they can't resist, such as A level teaching, small groups, free housing, higher pay . . . And it happens early in the course before the state sector adverts start appearing in the *TES*.

**T.B.**  That's wickedness of a high order, but we're working on a package that would offer a whole range of incentives to young teachers. There's all the cultural facilities in Birmingham – the Rep, the Symphony Hall and such like; we can coordinate a professional development programme; we need to look at subsidized housing and all the other benefits.

**R.C.W.**  However, I suspect what has actually made the biggest difference to Birmingham schools are your own statements about the importance of good teachers – your celebration of good teaching and where it's taking place and how to do it.

**T.B.** Yes, we have some excellent teachers. We need some equally excellent structures for them to work in. In an urban education system you need a collegiate academy, you need a University of the First Age which organizes extension enrichment opportunities and you need a virtual college. We need to make the nine minutes of experience a bit longer, and do something about the kids who are bunking off who don't even get five minutes. Then we'd stop wasting the talent we do.

We need to really look at the possibilities of ICT. If you think back to what teachers used to say in the days when they told stories and the book came along, they panicked. They thought, 'Bloody hell, when they've got books at home, they won't need me.' And the reaction to ICT is sometimes the same. But the opportunities it offers teachers to extend their teaching are enormous. ICT touches music, English, languages, history, everything. We're only in the foothills of what we can do with media-assisted learning. Never mind emailing or enriching the library, or word processing; there is so much more.

Recently I saw a thing called Autoskills, which is the next stage on from Success Maker. You know, how when you're watching kids playing 'Raiders' or whatever it is and they go from one level to another like lightning you think, 'How the hell do they do it as fast as they do?' I was watching a girl working on Autoskills in her school. She was 11 and her reading age had been 8 on entry to the school.

'Do you want to join in?' she said. 'I'm going to do a comprehension.' 'Really? What are they?' I replied. 'They're difficult, they are,' she says. 'You only get one chance at it; the machine never lets you have more than one go. They're what you call unseen.' 'Really?' I said. 'You must see them though?' And she laughed. 'OK, we'll have a go together.'

So she throws up this unseen comprehension and starts working on it. I'm doing it in my head. She's going like greased lighting and I'm labouring along a little behind. At the end it measured her for accuracy and speed. She was better than I was. What I saw happening was the programme elasticizing the cognitive process in a way that I can remember about some amazingly good episodes of learning for myself. It was happening in relation to both her level of skill and her conceptual understanding.

Which is why I say we're just in the foothills. With the skills of teachers who understand about teaching and learning, and with some of the systemic things in place that we've been talking about here, people will look back in 2020 and say it was now that the big break happened.

**R.C.W.** And you're in the 89th minute . . .

**T.B.** Yes, but there's extra time.

**R.C.W.** Thank you so much.

# 9

# Interview with Anita Higham OBE

Principal of Banbury School, Oxfordshire
1985–1998

**Roger Crombie White**   I'd like to start with your own experiences of school.
**Anita Higham**   I went to a convent preparatory school from the age of
4 until I was 9. Then my parents moved to Lancashire, and I went to
another convent preparatory school. From there, after I took my 11-plus,
I was given a place at a direct grant grammar school, as opposed to a
secondary modern or a secondary technical. I stayed there until I took
my O levels. At that time you had to be 15 on 1 September of the school
year in which you were going to do your O levels. I was only 14, so I had
to repeat my fifth year, and ended up taking O levels in 1953, the year
after A levels were first introduced.

My parents then moved to Berkshire and I went to an all-girls, maintained grammar school in Reading, where I took my A levels in 1955. So,
from the age of 4 until almost 19 I was in a girls' school within the
private or direct grant sector.
**R.C.W.**   Did you enjoy it?
**A.H.**   Enormously. I was happy at school. If ever I was ill enough to have
to stay away, which was fairly rare, I really didn't like it because I felt the
world was going on without me. I enjoyed it. But because I was five foot
eight when I was 11 and I was always very overweight for my age, I
couldn't conform physically to my peers. So I used always to sit at the
back of the class and was very quiet. I didn't have very much self-
confidence, nor did I have a huge number of friends, but that was to do
with my own personal development, not with the school.
**R.C.W.**   One of the threads running through what the young people talk
about is the importance of friends. The nature of the experience in primary and secondary schools is defined by the quality of friendships.
**A.H.**   Yes, absolutely. What I'm saying though is that I think I would have
had a problem wherever I was because I was so overweight. It may have

been worse if I'd not been in a convent school. I think I was very vulnerable. Mostly it was people outside the school who made comments, although I was once referred to by the PE teacher as the Rock of Gibraltar, because I couldn't manage things in the gymnasium.

**R.C.W.** Were your parents very much involved at that time?

**A.H.** They were always very keen supporters in terms of education. My mother would never buy my sister, brother or me anything outside of Christmas and birthdays unless it was a book. They both made a lot of sacrifices to give us a good education.

My father had left school at 14 and always had an enormous inferiority complex intellectually, although he worked his way up to an executive role with a large company. My mother had been one of the first cohort of young people to go to the municipal grammar school on a scholarship, just after the First World War. She was the only one of her brothers and sisters to do so. She did very well until two weeks before sitting her School Certificate when she was caught smoking at school and was expelled.

I never knew about this until I was in my first teaching post in a girls' school. I remember going home one weekend and telling my mother about a girl in my form who'd been caught smoking and had been suspended. She was extraordinarily bright, but very complex. Mother was doing the ironing in the kitchen when I told her this. She stopped and sat down. 'You've got to tell the head that she mustn't expel this girl. She mustn't send her away.' And then Mother told me what had happened to her. She never had a job and just helped out at home after that. But she was very supportive of us during our own time at school. I think she saw herself reflected in me as I pursued my own career in education. My parents would have been very proud to see me receive the OBE in 1996.

**R.C.W.** So from the girls' grammar school you went on to university?

**A.H.** I went to Nottingham to read French, with Latin as my subsidiary subject. However I was thrown out of the Honours school at the end of my second year. I spent too much time playing chess and, to quote Cleopatra, experiencing 'my salad days when I was green of judgement' rather than working. I consequently graduated with a pass degree!

Having graduated I then went to France, as an assistante in Marseille for a year, followed by a second year in Avignon. I investigated the possibilities of doing a Licence (the French BA equivalent) at the University of Aix-Marseille, and decided I would really work hard to get a Licence in order to make up for having made a mess of my first degree. Because it was a modular course, I was able to take time off in the middle to do a PGCE course at Cavendish Square, which was run by an order of nuns and attached to the London Institute of Education.

I think the idea of teaching had first been put in my head by the person who was my 'moral tutor' at Nottingham University, for whom I used to babysit. He also happened to run the careers service in the university. In my final year he asked me, 'What are you thinking of doing?' and I said, 'I don't really know. Perhaps the United Nations or the BBC.' 'Well,' he said, 'if you were teaching my daughter (who was then at Nottingham High School for Girls), I think you would be brilliant.' I suppose he'd sensed I'd be good, but I didn't feel drawn to teaching at that point. It came later, when I interrupted my Licence course to do the PGCE.

It took me eighteen months to finish my Licence in modern letters. I specialized in French, with Italian and English as my subsidiary subjects. I came out with very good grades or 'mentions' as they're called in French, and felt that I had finally justified my intellectual self. Then, although I still wasn't sure if I wanted to teach, I started applying for teaching jobs. I was offered all of the ones I applied for, all in girls' convent schools, and I was 'graciously pleased' to accept one of them where a friend of mine was teaching history. I didn't like the first fortnight and was thinking, 'What have I done?' when it just 'clicked' and I started to find it all so exciting. I began to get a sense of the chemistry between the teacher and the taught. I felt passionately about my teaching – more so as the years passed. I worked in that girls' independent convent school for five years. As a youngish teacher, very enthusiastic about her work, I soon established quite a standing in the school, but I soon knew it wasn't where I wanted to spend the rest of my working life.

**R.C.W.** Why was that?

**A.H.** My sister was at the London School of Economics at the time, and she and I shared a flat together in Kilburn in London. She would come back to the flat in the evening and talk about the lectures she'd gone to and the people she was meeting and the ideas that were around in the LSE at that time. For the first time in my life I started to question my Catholicism and what it meant to be a Christian. Added to this was the powerful influence of Existentialist philosophy, from having studied French. I felt passionately about that, and still do to this day. I believe that because you exist, you are morally obliged to engage with society; that's how you build up the very essence of who and what you are. You have to engage – you can't just talk about it – you have to act.

**R.C.W.** Which became one of the slogans of the '68 revolution?

**A.H.** Camus: '*Il faut agir.*' Sartre: '*La parole est aux actes.*' Camus and his writings about the meaning of love, and the pain and the suffering that goes into it had also profoundly influenced me. As a human being, you have no choice but to love, unless you choose to die. One of Camus's essays, called the Myth of Sisyphus, begins with the most important question: 'Shall I commit suicide or not?' Camus argues that, if you decide to commit suicide, then you've made one decision; but if you decide not to commit suicide, then you've decided that you have to engage. You have to make every effort to love, in the fullest sense of the word. I guess that is also what my Christianity means for me.

With that influence from existentialism in the background and the discussions with my sister, I realized that I couldn't go on working in the independent convent school too much longer. I thought about going to work in a primary school, because there was a lot of talk about teaching French at that level. I remember being interviewed for a school in Hampstead somewhere. I didn't get the job and I don't think I was right for it. I didn't know enough about how young children learn.

Then I thought of going into teacher training. I applied to a Catholic college of education that was being opened in Liverpool and was called for interview. However, at the same time, I was invited to interview for the post of senior mistress in a mixed comprehensive school in Bristol. The interviews were on adjacent days. I went to Bristol first. There were five other women applicants who had all worked in comprehensive schools. I thought, 'They won't appoint me. I've never taught boys and I've only ever worked with independent school girls from professional, wealthy backgrounds.' And lo and behold, they offered me the job! I said, 'Well, I've been called for an interview as a lecturer in French at a college of education in Liverpool and it's tomorrow.' Could I let them know the day after? I remember the LEA representative on the interviewing panel, replying, 'I think you would be of much greater value in a college of education if you'd spent a few years working in a place like this.'

The governors gave me two hours to make my mind up. I walked around the grounds of the school with the deputy head; I talked with people, and then I sat on my own, thinking, knowing I had to make up my mind. I decided to accept the job, and the rest, as they say, is history.

**R.C.W.** This is very interesting. Your own education was quite privileged and you start teaching in a girls' independent school. You have a sister who is sharing ideas and experiences that resonate with thinking from your time in France. Then the rest of your teaching life is spent in mainstream comprehensives, some of which are exceedingly challenging. You could easily have done something quite different.

**A.H.** Oh yes. I was once asked to be a serious applicant for the principal's job at Cheltenham Ladies College. I could have imagined myself doing that job.

Because of my existential philosophy, I have this passionate feeling that every child has a right to learn. Every child has a right to be treated with dignity and has a right to as much as you can offer. Even though they have different needs, they are all of the same value.

It started as an existential belief – it became a political belief.

**R.C.W.** How?

**A.H.** It was born out of thinking about what I was doing. When I left the girls' independent school in Hertfordshire and went to Bristol, I desperately felt that I needed to start formal learning again. I signed up to do an

Advanced Diploma and then a Masters Degree in the School of Education at Bristol. I was hugely influenced by Professor Ben Morris and the readings I did during that time. I also joined a course run on Saturdays by Elizabeth Richardson which opened another world for me, a much more extended world of trying to understand who and what I was as a person, both in the working context and otherwise.

As an adolescent I'd been so repressed that I hadn't done any of the things that people did in their adolescence. I didn't have the self-confidence. I thought I was hugely unattractive. I thought that nobody liked me or would want to be friendly with me, so that I had to fight to exist on my own, because I was just not of value, in the deep sense of the word. Throughout my adolescent period those were very powerful feelings and influences.

It wasn't until I was in my late twenties that I found the woman in myself, and found the person in myself was not such an unattractive person after all. But throughout my adolescence and my early twenties I had really developed my intellectual side as a means whereby I could connect with people, because I'd found that I did engage with people intellectually in a very exciting and interesting way. Others would be engaging sexually or engaging in a social way, but I did it through the intellectual mode.

And so, as a result of the courses at Bristol University, I came to a much more profound understanding of and insight into what education was all about. One of the most important things I learnt from Ben Morris, which I've often quoted, is that the professional person is the person who has an ability to reflect upon what they are doing and actually to do something about it. It's like Sartre, '*La parole est aux actes.*' In French, '*la parole*' is the spoken word, 'le mot' is the written word. You can't just sit and do nothing if you feel it. It's what you do in this life which matters and counts.

Through my subsequent work with the Tavistock and the Grubb Institutes I learned a lot about authority, the way in which men and women work in organizations and the way in which people use or misuse authority in their working context. The more that I reflected on my daily experiences in school and read, the more I understood about what a school community had to be about, or had to try to do. Very often adults put children down because they have so many hang-ups themselves; they don't allow children to start being persons; and they can become frightened of them, of course. If you engage with a child as a person, that makes so many more demands on you as a person; many teachers find this difficult.

**R.C.W.**   One of the things that the girls and the boys stress here as important is relationships with teachers. What they want is respect. They don't like being treated as Year 7 when they are in Year 11.

**A.H.** Yes, they hate being patronized. They want to be taken seriously. I've always felt passionately about the rights of children to be treated as persons, to be taught properly, to experience a full and varied curriculum. They need to feel valued as persons. That is very profound in me, perhaps because I have had the experience of often not feeling valued. That feeling still lives in me; it's something I still have to work with.

**R.C.W.** In order for teachers to value children, they need to be valued too.

**A.H.** Yes, exactly. But they also need to value themselves. If you don't value yourself, then you can't rely on other people doing it. I always remember the woman who taught me Latin, Miss Clough, asking what I was going to do in the sixth form. And I said I'd like to do English, French and Latin, but I didn't know if I was good enough. Miss Clough replied, 'Anita, the world places upon us the value which we place on ourselves. Never forget that.' And she was absolutely right. She was telling me something very profound and it took many years before I fully understood what she was saying.

**R.C.W.** In your booklet for SHA, '*Tomorrow's School*' (Higham 1995) you offer a vision of how schooling ought to be, and you describe the current model as still being as it was in the nineteenth century.

**A.H.** Yes, we are, I believe, a hundred and thirty years out of date. Very little has changed in the style and structure of schools. We are in the death throes of secondary schools as we know them. We can no longer rely on a model whose objective was to serve the needs of a flourishing Victorian nation through the education of the able sons of its middle and professional classes. It was typically male, classical, middle-class and clean. 'Getting one's hands dirty' didn't feature. The curriculum and style of teaching were precisely geared to ensure that universities would have their necessary supply of researchers, dons and professors. It's what I have referred to as 'the failed physics professor model'.

Now, still using this model, we seek to educate the whole spectrum of young people, from those with severe learning difficulties through to the most gifted – girls as well as boys – and all of them are required by statute to be in full-time education to the later phase of adolescence.

It isn't so much a curriculum issue as a structural issue, although there are some important changes that could be made in curriculum terms. There are core curriculum headings that we need to consider which are not identified by the national curriculum – boundaries, values and personal responsibility.

For example, I feel deeply that it is a whole person who comes daily into school – not just a piece of brain or a body of limbs. Consequently the spiritual dimension of the curriculum is crucial. The arts (music, dance, drama, and the visual arts), together with good quality tutoring, physical education and a student social management structure (one which seeks to develop appropriate behaviour rather than the dependency much beloved of generations of teachers in order to control students) are all essential elements of the learning community's spiritual life. They are the crucial means for learning about boundaries, values and personal responsibility.

I am also deeply committed to ensuring that the public understanding of science be achieved via the quality of science and technology learning offered to the young, such that they be sufficiently well informed to make very important and even moral decisions in their adult lives. My definition of technology is that it is the application of the laws and principles of the pure sciences and of mathematics to enable the man-made world to come fully into being. These are all further dimensions to the essential learning about values and personal responsibility.

**R.C.W.**　Have you seen the RSA document, *Opening Minds* (Bayliss 1999), with its emphasis on competences rather than subjects – some of which correlate closely with the core curriculum headings you've just mentioned?

**A.H.**　Yes, the RSA materials offer a pragmatic vision. I agree with it, although I think the vision needs more warmth – it needs to reflect a more passionate affection and respect for children as persons.

**R.C.W.**　It also highlights the role of ICT. This is something that you draw attention to in your own booklet, with reference to Tim Brighouse and Michael Barber's work on the University of the First Age in Birmingham and David Hargreaves's ideas in *The Mosaic of Learning* (1995) for differentiated and specialized learning centres.

**A.H.**　But these ICT developments, exciting as they are, are really just tools. They are no different in essence from the piece of chalk and the blackboard. It's just that they are different sorts of tools, part of our present revolutionary world, necessary for achieving what it is you want children to achieve in terms of their own dignity as twenty-first-century adults. The critical component is the quality of teachers. We are in danger of 'killing off' the very asset that is central to any effective structural change – namely, good teachers. Alongside changes to the pattern and location of schooling, I would argue that our most important task is to enhance and elevate the professional role of teachers.

Teachers must be enabled to make the interdependent connection between the nation's 'wealth creators' and themselves, the nation's 'citizen creators'. The interdependence between education and the world of business/industry is a crucial element, too long ignored by both, who so often snipe destructively at one another, from the opposite sides of the same highway, which is taking the direction *both* need to follow.

Teachers need to feel valued and empowered and need to be able to guide young people effectively through the choices they face. My own education gave me an enormous number of choices; which is why I feel so passionately that, if you don't enable children to achieve their potential, particularly with regard to accreditation, then you are depriving them of choices which enable them to explore how to be fuller human beings. They may not choose to be fuller or even better human beings, but that's up to them. I guess I've been influenced by reading Paulo Freire and his belief that teaching somebody to read and to write enfranchises them. People have a right to be given the right to make choices.

**R.C.W.** Doesn't that lead you into the political arena? For example, if you are running a comprehensive school as you were until very recently, there are serious funding constraints, and it's possible to make unfavourable comparisons with the independent sector in terms of the opportunities and choices available for young people. Some of the sixth formers here have made a comparison with one of the independent schools close by in terms of resourcing. The resourcing of their comprehensive school seemed impoverished compared to the independent school . . . and they were annoyed about this. They felt it was unfair.

**A.H.** I feel very strongly that there is a huge educational apartheid in this country. I remember once using that phrase with a group of independent head teachers who did not like it at all. This apartheid is all tied up with the English class system – English rather than British I guess. It's profoundly destructive and any government that doesn't understand that and isn't prepared to work at that really doesn't get my vote.

When the assisted places thing first came in, I felt it was an insult to those of us working in comprehensive schools. It was basically saying that comprehensive schools aren't good enough for bright children and that those bright children had to be given the opportunity to go elsewhere. I know from experience that this is not true.

**R.C.W.** Educational apartheid is an emotive phrase.

**A.H.** I choose it deliberately; I choose it knowingly.

**R.C.W.** But what would you say to a parent who says, 'I want the best for my child? How can you deny me the opportunity to buy into the private sector?'

**A.H.** There's always a huge dichotomy between dealing with the needs of an individual and the needs of the wider society. When you are dealing with an individual couple of parents all you can say is, 'You must do what you believe is in the best interests of your own child.' When you are looking at the needs of a whole nation or a local authority area though, and you're looking at a timespan of ten, twenty, thirty years hence, you have to look at it somewhat differently. It's very complex.

I might try and persuade you as parents that the richest resource that the school offered your child was not so much the swimming pool, the music centre, the small classes, or whatever, but was actually the richness of the mixture of children from a wide range of backgrounds, and how they managed themselves – and how they learnt to manage to be members of society because of the way the school was organized and managed them. If you didn't want to be persuaded of that, I'd feel sad about it, but I'd respect your choice.

It's for governments and local education authorities to tackle the issue of educational apartheid. I acknowledge that using such a phrase can be a bit threatening though.

**R.C.W.**  Well it is, but it's an accurate description of what's happening and we have to make some choices about the kind of society we want, and the kind of society we want our children to inherit. Most people would say they do not want a segregated and divided society where a few rather well-off people are hiding behind fences that are 20 feet high to keep out those who have very little. We need to ask people how they – we – are going to prevent that happening?

**A.H.**  The difficulty is that there are some people who may very well want a segregated society. A child can go to Banbury School and get straight As at GCSE, then four A levels with grade As – and I can think of some in this category – and go to either Oxford or Cambridge. So why doesn't every parent want to send their child to a school like Banbury, of which there are large numbers throughout the country? The thing they say they want (good exam results) is deliverable and achievable there, together with the social richness of a diverse community of students.

The truth is that there are other reasons why parents choose private schools.

I was at a meeting recently with a number of people who I know send their children to private schools. At one point I said, 'I think that a lot of parents use the private system because they want to buy their children into a network.' There was a stunned silence. The chairman took a deep breath, and I said, 'Discuss!' It's quite true for some parents. If you want to buy your child into a network, then you might say, 'It's worth spending £15,000 a year if I can get him into Eton.'

The solution is to make state schools so very good that any alternative is hardly worth considering. To do this we need to search out and articulate a new direction for secondary education – how and where we locate it, how to form and shape the role of teachers, how to structure their working day and year, how to shape the curriculum, the pattern of the school year, the potential of ICT – all the issues I raised in *Tomorrow's School* (1995). We must design new models, find new styles, clarify our values and beliefs and try to find the courage to work with them. The young have a right to demand this of us.

**R.C.W.**  Thank you very much, Anita.

# 10

# Interview with Professor Richard Pring

Director of Department of Educational Studies, Oxford University

**Roger Crombie White** What primary and secondary schools did you go to?

**Richard Pring** I went to primary school in Sheffield, until I passed the 11-plus examination, and then moved to a Catholic grammar school. At the age of 13 I decided I wanted to become a priest so I moved to a junior seminary. From there, at the age of 17, I went out to the English College in Rome where I remained for three years. When I came back to England the first time after those three years for a holiday, I decided not to carry on and chose instead to study philosophy at University College in London under A. J. Ayer.

**R.C.W.** Why the change in direction from training for the priesthood to studying philosophy?

**R.P.** During the three years in Rome the philosophy was based very much upon Thomas Aquinas. It was all in Latin, we were examined in Latin, and the lectures were in Latin. Just about the only English book that I came across in the library at the English College was A.J. Ayer's *Language, Truth and Logic* (Ayer 1936). At that time it was an exceedingly popular philosophical book and deeply influential. Its main thesis is that the meaning of a proposition is its mode of verification. Since, according to the book, there are only two such modes, namely by reference to the principle of contradiction or by empirical evidence, all other kinds of propositions, including those of theology, morality, politics and so on, are basically meaningless.

Studying philosophy with Ayer was a very significant part of my education because he was a very good teacher, and his philosophical way of thinking was something I felt deeply committed to. I was constantly trying to find a way out of various holes, which were dug by this very strict application of the principle of verification.

**R.C.W.** And after you graduated?

**R.P.** I joined the Civil Service, which was another crucial part of my education, particularly in terms of communication skills. As an assistant principal, one devilled for a higher level civil servant. One had to learn how to produce arguments very clearly and succinctly, for different audiences, anticipating how the next person – be it a higher up civil servant or the Secretary of State – would be able to take on that argument. So I think that was a very important part of education in terms of communication skills.

**R.C.W.** How has your own schooling experience shaped your belief in the importance of comprehensive education?

**R.P.** There were two streams in my primary school. Of the top stream of fifty-odd pupils, all but two passed their 11-plus and went to the grammar school. Of the bottom stream, all but two failed the 11-plus. In effect, therefore, selection was taking place when the two groups were first streamed, at the age of 9, on a very arbitrary basis. So what has made an indelible mark upon my own memory and my own thinking has been the incredible unfairness of what was purported at the time to be an objective way of dividing out those who were capable of a grammar school education and those who were not.

The grammar school also had two forms, divided according to whether you were capable of doing Latin or not – in which case you did art. So only a small number were looked on as really capable of a grammar school education. Even in the grammar school, those in the B stream were regarded as rather stupid, and I look back with shame at how I took on those attitudes – feeling rather superior to those who actually failed and went to the secondary moderns or were placed in the B stream of the grammar school. One thing that I have remained passionate about is the injustice of early selection. I don't think it can be justified at all. Hence my commitment to a comprehensive system of education.

**R.C.W.** And how about your views about the process of teaching and learning?

**R.P.** At the primary stage we were taught fairly formally, which worked for me, particularly in relation to mathematics and literacy. My grasp of the tools to talk about language goes back to this period and I would be critical of an education that denied people these tools and the capacity to engage in basic mental arithmetic. But I'm aware that for a lot of young people their education was dependent on fear rather than developing a love for the subject. In grammar school for instance, we were taught by a very large Irishman, who beat Latin into us, such that we went to school in fear and trembling, learning it on the tramcar (which fortunately was a very long journey and left a long time for doing our homework). There were a lot who had Latin beaten out of them, because they constantly made mistakes with their declensions and their irregular verbs.

**R.C.W.** Did you ever find learning rather difficult?

**R.P.** Yes, of course. Because I was a fairly logical child, unless I saw the point of something, I would worry away at it. I just couldn't accept things simply on authority. And I remember a particular time during physics – in which I had understood everything that had gone on for the previous six months – where the teacher just shifted over a point, which I didn't really understand. What followed seemed to be unintelligible. I had no grasp of the presuppositions. Thereafter science very quickly became a question of learning things by heart rather than through understanding the underpinning ideas. All it required was someone to have explained those ideas.

This all made more sense to me when I came across Bruner's writings. He argued that it was essential for teachers to identify those key ideas, without which you don't really grasp the subject matter, without which everything seems incomprehensible. The essence of teaching is to actually put across those key ideas in a way that is intelligible to people at different levels of their own development. According to Bruner even the most complex and abstract ideas can be put across in a way that is intelligible to children at a very young age. That is one of the essential ingredients of good teaching.

There's a myth about knowledge increasing so rapidly that it's very difficult to keep up with it. If you think in Bruner's terms, knowledge isn't increasing rapidly at all – it's changing. Rather than learn lots and lots of knowledge, we need to grasp those key ideas without which the experience becomes unintelligible. The National Curriculum has not been really thought through in these terms, but rather in terms of coverage of material. To take an example from history, what ideas were at the core of the American Declaration of Independence, and the subsequent revolution? What were those key ideas without which we really don't understand this complexity of events?

The other essential ingredient is being taught by people who love their subject. Some of my most vivid memories are learning Latin and Roman history in my junior seminary where I had some brilliant teachers, like Father Sweeney who read Ovid and Horace and Virgil for sheer pleasure. Roman history still retains a kind of intellectual delight. I almost look forward to retiring so that I can go back to it and study it again. The lesson from that period of my life is that inspiration, being taught by somebody who loves the ideas, loves the subject, is absolutely crucial. I think one should be prepared to sacrifice coverage of lots of subjects, in order to ensure that one is taught by people who believe in it, love it and convey passion and love for what they have.

**R.C.W.** Do you have many regrets about your own schooling?

**R.P.** Not really. I had an exceedingly happy childhood. One thing I do regret is that I must have been a massive sacrifice for my parents. At the age of 17 I went off to Rome not to be seen again (except once, when they came out for a very brief holiday) for three years. Having had three children of my own, who are all well past 17, I think the idea of saying goodbye to them for that period of time would have been a fairly intolerable sacrifice. But in those days one's parents did whatever the Bishop said should be done. If the Bishop decided I should go to Rome because I was rather good at Latin, then off I went to Rome, but it must have been very painful for my parents.

**R.C.W.** How did this quite privileged, selective experience lead you into engagement with comprehensive education?

**R.P.** It was during the time I was assistant principal at the Ministry of Education, and involved with the Curriculum Study Group, which had just been formed. This was in 1963 under that brilliant civil servant, Derek Morell, who remains one of the most inspiring figures in my thinking about education.

This was the period of the setting up of the Schools Council and I became very interested in the educational rationale behind this. There was a kind of mood in the Civil Service at that time, a very buoyant mood – a feeling that with time we would have such a damn good state educational system that nobody would bother to send their children to private school. There was also a real questioning of the value of the 11-plus. So I became very interested in education. And since I am very much a people's person – that is, I like mixing with people and sitting at a desk isn't something which I enjoy too much – I decided that I would train to be a teacher to work in a comprehensive school.

**R.C.W.** Why a comprehensive school in particular?

**R.P.** I think I was deeply committed to the values underpinning comprehensive education. I was fully aware of the inadequacies of selection at the age of 11. If you operate selection, then there are two things that you've got to be sure about. First, you've got to be sure that you can distinguish two relatively homogeneous groups, fitted for very different kinds of education in the grammar school or the secondary modern. That assumes there are two quite clearly distinguishable aims of education – which, to my mind, is nonsense. Second, even if that were the case, you need the instruments through which you could accurately make that kind of selection. Although the 11-plus was an improvement on selecting people as a result of influence or money, it was in fact a very blunt instrument indeed.

**R.C.W.** Was your experience of comprehensive schooling all good?

**R.P.** No, not at all. What was wrong with the system at that time – and I think this would be the case in many, many schools – was that there was so much freedom for individual teachers to do what they liked. For example, in my first school there was no scheme of work in any of the subjects that I was teaching. It was very much up to me what I taught

– without any kind of plan that would lead them on the next year into a deeper understanding of the subject.

How can one teach like that? One ought to be able to identify the key ideas which can be reinforced and deepened and which govern the curriculum planning. Nowadays of course schools do have proper schemes of work and teachers work within this framework. The National Curriculum has helped that to happen.

**R.C.W.** What were the good things?

**R.P.** There were plenty of inspirational teachers, who conveyed a set of values which I think you would not have found in other parts of society at that time – teachers who were deeply committed to bringing all children on irrespective of gender or race for instance. To see the moral commitment of these people was very inspiring. Some of them were just quite brilliant. And that brilliance very rarely gets acknowledged outside schools. You still see it today.

Moreover, a great number of teachers were meeting regularly in their subject groups and were doing some immense thinking about the curriculum. The Humanities Curriculum Project is a good example – not just for the materials it produced for schools, but for the subgroups it generated all over the country where teachers came together to talk about the role of humanities in education. Much of this happened out of hours.

If you took teaching seriously it was a very exciting and intellectually demanding profession to be in. One felt inspired to be part of it . . . and I think that helped maintain what I call the comprehensive ideal – an ideal whereby all people count, irrespective of background, colour, race, creed or whatever. And I believe there's enough creativity and evaluation and moral purpose amongst teachers to make such an ideal work.

**R.C.W.** Did your commitment to comprehensive education extend to the choice you made for your own children?

**R.P.** Both my wife and I were deeply committed to comprehensive schools. We also believed that the comprehensive system would not work unless people demonstrated their belief in it by sending their own children to it. My children experienced a quality to learning that they would not have received had they gone into a private system. They came across teachers who were exceedingly good, very dedicated, very caring, and they came to appreciate working and learning to live with children who came from disadvantaged homes, who hadn't got much money, who had real difficulties, who they got to know and befriend – whom they would never have got to know otherwise. All my children are quite classless, insofar as they do not have any prejudice in terms of social class, race or gender. They have turned out to be very well-rounded, well-adjusted, balanced people. They are very independent minded. They are able to form good relationships with people. They are all well qualified. They are all earning a living. Those comprehensive schools that they went to in the formative parts of their lives have been very successful.

One of the great sadnesses though is that a lot of their friends at primary school disappeared off to private schools, reinforcing this socially divided society, which we have, and which continues to be reinforced by a select, private system of education.

**R.C.W.**  Do you still feel optimistic about comprehensive education?

**R.P.**  A lot depends upon what comprehensive schools you are talking about. I'd be more than happy for my children to go to any of the comprehensive schools which I am dealing with through our Internship Scheme. They tend to be well-run places and they achieve good results. But a lot of schools referred to as comprehensive schools are only that in name alone. They are part of a wider selective system, with 161 grammar schools in existence, which affect approximately 500 comprehensive schools, turning many of them into de facto secondary moderns.

I think one has got to be very careful in saying, 'Would you send your children to comprehensive schools?' Most of the ones that I come across I would be very happy for them to go to, but obviously there are some I wouldn't. But that is partly because governments, this one included, have failed to provide an adequate supply of teachers. Many comprehensive schools are not going to be able to attract sufficiently good qualified teachers. There's an exponential decline in people wanting to teach things like maths, physics and so on, and increasingly, these relatively few people are going to be poached by the independent sector. Therefore there is going to be a great impoverishment in terms of the actual subject knowledge in a lot of comprehensive schools, and that is exceedingly worrying.

What also worries me is that there's a tangible decline in the morale of staff as they are constantly battered by criticism from people who ought to know better. The way ahead must be to look back – not to everything that went on in the sixties and seventies, because there was a lot that was quite shameful – but to the really good things that went on and remind ourselves of the immense creativity and moral sense of purpose which is there in the teaching profession, and to tap into it. If only the politicians were to recognize it and not maintain this anal-retentive approach in which they feel they've got to control everything from the centre instead of handing over responsibility to teachers.

**R.C.W.**  So what needs to happen?

**R.P.**  First, the government needs to provide more opportunities for teachers to work together in their subject associations, with sufficient time and adequate resources to enable them to think about, talk about and plan the curriculum. In many parts of the country now you don't have any Teachers' Centres – places where teachers are able to come together professionally. That is something which ought to be recreated. In order to do this, the government would need to take much more seriously the importance of giving teachers the opportunity to recharge their batteries and to think professionally. You shouldn't expect people to be teaching for thirty years without the time or the scope to really rethink what they're doing. It's no good relying on teachers using time in their holidays or in the evenings for such things, because good teachers are now spending most of their evenings marking and preparing for the next day. As long as there's that relentless and continual load upon teachers, they are not going to be able to relax about the job and actually think about it.

Second, the government must be much less prescriptive about the amount of subject detail it requires teachers to cover. There ought to be much more support for that part of the professional judgement of a teacher which says, 'This group of pupils needs to go deeper in the subject, not skate rather superficially in order to cover the National Curriculum syllabus.' It goes back to what I described at the beginning, with reference to my own experience, about the significance of covering less breadth but being inspired by what you do cover. And making sure that what you do cover gets at those key ideas that are at the heart of any subsequent learning and understanding.

Third, one has to do something about ensuring that academically able people want to come into teaching. Teaching has to be sold as a career and not just as a job where people are treated like unskilled labourers who go here, there and everywhere, instead of as some of our most precious resources that really need to be managed, from the time they opt to come into teaching.

Careers officers need to be able to say to young people, 'Look, if you go in for teaching, this is where you can expect to be in five years.' But one of the difficulties under LMS and the decline of LEAs is that we've now got a very fragmented system, so we are not able to manage young people coming into teaching. And therefore, when these very able young people come along, they are then in a sort of lottery as to where they are going to teach, what they are going to teach, will they be able to teach A level or not. I think that is something which has really got to be addressed.

**R.C.W.** How would you manage them?

**R.P.** Firstly, all student teachers including those doing a BA or BEd degree, not just PGCE students, need a proper salary right from the time they join . . . in the way that nurses do, in the way that apprentice lawyers do. Students have to make a major financial sacrifice in order to be a teacher – and it isn't going to actually pay them that much when they qualify. I'm not saying the starting salary is very bad, but for many people who want to go into teaching, it doesn't justify the actual outlay of all their expenses whilst they're training.

Secondly, when a teacher says, 'Look, this is the area I want to teach and these are the kind of subjects I want to teach at A level,' there ought to be some mechanism which enables LEAs to guarantee them this kind of opportunity. Each year I lose brilliant young teachers who want to teach in the comprehensive system. I lose them to the independent sector, not because they particularly want the independent sector, but because the independent sector is able to say in December or January, 'We'll offer you a job. Secondly, we're going to offer you A level teaching. And thirdly, we're going to provide you with better conditions, possibly cheap housing.'

We want something like that to be offered at the regional level for people who want to teach in comprehensive schools. We need to be able to say to people when they start their training, 'We can guarantee you a job and we can make sure that you are going to be able to afford to come and teach in this expensive kind of area. What's the sort of school you want? Right, you want A level – we'll make sure that you get A level teaching.' So in many ways it could be managed. It's not going to be easy in the kind of fragmented and competitive system that has now been established. But unless one does do that there's going to be a gradual bleeding out of the profession of very able people.

**R.C.W.**   And do we need to be thinking about the actual structure of schools and the organization of the learning process? Do these need to change as well?

**R.P.**   Oh certainly! Such as the principle of the school being rigidly organized between certain hours. I think we are already seeing that particular wall being breached. Of course there have been examples in the past, like the Cambridge village colleges, which were centres of learning, involving the youth service and adult education service working in tandem with schools. Adults were able to sit alongside the young people in lessons. Teachers would serve both the youth service and the schools and the same youngsters might be taking part in both. There have been lots of examples where schools are seen as centres for a whole range of community activities.

We also ought to be thinking much more carefully about how technology can be utilized to enable much greater differentiation and give individuals more control of their own learning pace. Technology opens up lots of possibilities for radical approaches, which have not been properly explored.

**R.C.W.**   Like what?

**R.P.**   Although you need a school as a physical centre in which activities can be organized, and where people can come if they wish – where there are proper laboratories and proper technology – we can explore the possibilities for learning within the community. I think that the view of the school as a kind of monastery, where all learning is contained within its walls, needs to be actually questioned.

There are so many resources in the community of people who, under the guidance of teachers, would be able to help. These ideas have been explored before. Within the framework of TVEI (Technical and Vocational Education Initiative) for instance (which started off in 1982 and finished about 1990) there was some unbelievably exciting and innovative work in which the pupils were involved with employers in the community in a whole range of different kinds of projects – in which the world of work was linked with the school. It was a time when teachers were given their hand in really being able to experiment and test things out without feeling terrified the whole time that they were going to be seen as failures.

The trouble is that, with what happened in 1988 and thereafter, it's as if the world began at that point. What is lacking in the minds of educational planners is a memory, which goes back to the very good things that happened before 1988 such as through TVEI and the Schools Council. There are many good examples where the rich resources of the community, with its enormous wisdom and knowledge, have been drawn in under the guidance of teachers. The possibilities of the new technology have yet to be exploited as well.

**R.C.W.**  In the past you have expressed concerns about the privatization of the state system. Do you see the continued existence of the private school sector as a problem for the state sector?

**R.P.**  Well, I think it is a problem because the quality of the local comprehensive school depends upon having a range of talents and well-motivated young people. And if those disappear off to the independent sector, then it becomes even more difficult for the state system. However, for the first time in our history we have a Prime Minister and Permanent Secretary who send their children to the comprehensive system, and we have a Secretary of State who has done so. I think there is a deep commitment to make the state system work. I believe you are never going to get a properly resourced and decent state system until the people who are running the country send their children there. We are moving in that direction and that gives me a certain amount of hope.

**R.C.W.**  Thank you very much.

# 11

# Interview with Dr Nick Tate

Headmaster of Winchester College
(and chief executive of Qualifications and
Curriculum Authority until summer 2000)

**Roger Crombie White**   Can we start with your own experiences of primary
and secondary schools?
**Nick Tate**   I had a pretty standard state elementary education. Very large
classes, very heavy concentration on the three Rs. Hardly a broad and balanced curriculum. I don't remember any PE or games or music. It gave me
a very sound grounding in mental arithmetic and basic aspects of literacy,
which has stood me in good stead. I'm grateful for that, although it makes
me highly intolerant of people who can't spell and punctuate. However,
the broadening of the imagination largely came from home and outside-
school contacts rather than school itself. Obviously this was partly denoted
by the fact that, having been given the grounding in literacy by those
schools, one was able to move on and begin to educate oneself in that way.
   Secondary school was a couple of fairly traditional grammar schools –
one mixed, the other a boys' grammar school, of a highly streamed, highly
traditional, highly exam-focused kind, but with some very stimulating
individual members of staff, who gave me a glimpse of what it was to be
an educated adult, and impressed me and made me want to be something
like that myself.
**R.C.W.**   You mean educated adult or a teacher?
**N.T.**   Educated adult. I'm particularly grateful to some of my grammar
school teachers for giving me a sense of what learning, knowledge and
scholarship did for one in terms of a breadth of vision, in making one an
interesting person, and in giving one a sense that there were all sorts of
ever-opening vistas to be explored. They didn't just enable me to do well
in exams (and I did very well in exams – I'm grateful for that as well), but
they really gave me a sense of what a well-read and informed person was
in the traditional literary sense. I found that very attractive and I wanted
to be one of those people myself.

**R.C.W.** So, did that influence what you chose to do?

**N.T.** Yes, I think it did. It influenced me to specialize in the arts and to become particularly interested in history and to read history at university. It also encouraged me to feel that my education was more than simply following the programmes that were laid down for examinations, degree courses and so on. I felt I ought to do something about my gross ignorance of lots of aspects of history that I'd not studied as part of the school and university courses. I felt I really ought to become better read in French literature, Spanish literature, American literature, and to read all the great Russian novels, and the great philosophers and all those sorts of things. I picked up a sense of both aspiration and enormous deficiency on my part. I hadn't read Tolstoy and I didn't know anything about Pascal, and I was very conscious from quite an early age that I really must do something about it.

**R.C.W.** The feeling of deficiency you mean?

**N.T.** Yes. I remember on one occasion looking at some massive historical tome, about one thousand five hundred pages in length. Half the periods I hadn't studied. And I remember thinking, I'll never, never do it. I shall never be able to read all this and understand all this. It's too much . . . But, you know, it wasn't a negative feeling. It really was very positive.

I frequently hear the comment from Oxford and Cambridge tutors that there isn't the breadth of interest and the desire in their students to sit up all night reading Pascal and Tolstoy and so on. When I went (and I'm talking now about the sort of child that I was, which was precociously and successfully academic), they were more mixed-ability universities – partly because they took lots of people who had connections. In some ways that was actually a good thing, because you had a genuine range of people. Nowadays you've probably got brighter people at traditional universities like Oxford and Cambridge, because they are more careful about their selection. Many people there these days have got three As, four As, five As, ten A stars at GCSE and that sort of thing – incredibly, formidably bright. Yet some of them aren't educated in the sense of having a passion for knowledge. Within a couple of years of leaving university they can be earning forty-five thousand as a management consultant and probe problems analytically in a most impressive way, but I don't always sense a thirst for learning.

**R.C.W.** Your reference to passion resonates with something Richard Pring says about how his own interest in ancient history was fuelled by a teacher who read Ovid and Virgil for sheer pleasure.

**N.T.** The passion is very important. I am attracted to people who have some sort of passion, whether it's for Byzantine history or the Coptic Church or butterflies or early garden design, or something. I feel there is something lacking in people who don't have that. Lots of people seem one-dimensional. They're super-nice people, with all the social skills and the communication skills, but there isn't a deep passion for anything. I don't know what drives them. I don't know, at the end of the day, what really matters to them.

This is one of the things that worry me sometimes with all the emphasis on lifelong learning. I don't think we sufficiently define what kind of learning it is and what the learning is for. Lifelong learning is seen as a good thing. But there are all sorts of different types of lifelong learning. One is the kind of lifelong learning that you need for employability and for job satisfaction and for effectiveness in work. Another is the kind of learning that you need to enable you to be a decent friend, parent, partner, citizen and all those sorts of things. And then, there is the cultivation of the mind and the soul and all of that. Quite often though it's the last of these that tends to get forgotten. Yet that was the vision of the educated person that I grew up with.

**R.C.W.** So now, as chief executive of QCA, responsible for the bigger vision, what drives the reshaping of the curriculum?

**N.T.** There are a lot of things that drive it, including preparation for citizenship and parental, social roles, as well as employability, which is very important. I wouldn't want to downplay that. But I think at the heart of the liberal education tradition is a desperate search to try and define what it is to be a human being and how you want to spend your life and what matters and what your values are – and all those sorts of things. Without that, there is something deficient.

It can take many different forms, but fundamentally education is about people making some kind of sense of their brief, transitory, contingent lives and not just muddling through. I don't know the answer, but it means that you wrestle and you struggle. For me it's partly a Christian thing in that, traditionally, the Christian view of life was that you were here to struggle towards some kind of perfection. You would never actually reach it, but you were struggling towards something in this life and towards something in the next life. So there is a sense of being driven. Laid on top of that for me – as a product of a highly literary education – is a sense that one should aspire to some extent to be a bit like Tolstoy or Pascal or Proust or Shakespeare – one's heroes who actually spent their lives engaging with these issues, trying to make sense of these things, trying to impose order on the chaos that surrounds our lives. If you don't participate in that to some extent and feel some kind of passion about it, then you are rather deficient as a human being.

**R.C.W.** The rhetoric of that is very fine, but what does it mean in curriculum terms? I remember Professor Wall, at the London Institute, once saying, 'The curriculum is just the fig leaf; it hides what's important.' Is the curriculum something of a straitjacket? Does it inhibit passion?

**N.T.** Well, I'm not sure it's the curriculum that does that necessarily. It could be the pressures on the curriculum and the pressures on teaching and learning approaches that come from examination requirements. Examinations inevitably impose some curricular constraints. But they don't have to inhibit passion. And if the curriculum does straitjacket, then it's failing.

One of the pieces of genuine news about the GCSE results this year concerns the massive increase in entries for the GCSE short course in religious education. This has been partly driven by schools that have received negative Ofsted reports about non-compliance with RE, so it's schools wanting to be law-abiding, with heads of RE saying, 'Look, you're going to get into trouble if you don't do something about this paragraph in the Ofsted report. Here is a way of actually motivating young people to get a certificate – which also counts towards the league tables.'

However, buried in that are some fantastic GCSE short course syllabuses, which are more than just religion. Sometimes religion is not even the major element; it's the ethics, it's the philosophy. We played a major role in working with the examination boards in developing and improving these. They are hugely popular, and they are encouraging young people to engage with some deeply significant and philosophical issues. No-one reaches the age of 14 or 15 without having had thoughts about death and the purpose of life, and these courses provide ways of shaping their thoughts and helping them to think through the important issues. There is a real resurgence of engagement with ethics and philosophy as a result of this. So that's an example of curricular change enabling people to address values and principles. Where the education system prevents this happening it may have as much to do with the nature of the teaching and learning process, as with the curriculum itself. Certainly pre-14 the teaching and learning process isn't determined by the statutory curriculum.

**R.C.W.** So is there something about the construction of Key Stage 4 that makes it more difficult to engage with what you refer to as the liberal education tradition?

**N.T.** The number of GCSEs that young people take at 16 has a bearing on this. Interestingly it's often far higher in state schools than in independent schools, where perhaps they don't feel quite the same pressures. Many of them genuinely think, 'Well, actually, there is more to 14–16 education than just doing vast numbers of GCSEs. There are lots of other extra-curricular activities that we don't want to see squeezed out – which develop character and motivation and those kinds of things.'

So I'm very distrustful of those who think that the solution to these problems lies largely in dramatically cutting back on curricular requirements, dismantling the curriculum, moving to multidisciplinary structures rather than disciplinary structures. I think a lot can be done through the current curriculum, especially if there is a sharper sense of why subjects are on the curriculum.

**R.C.W.** And you see that understanding of the rationale as key?

**N.T.** I've always felt that if we could develop a clearer and more shared view of why we're doing certain things – in this very fundamental sense of what kind of educated person are we trying to create – then we could actually be much more relaxed about the curriculum requirements and teachers could freely choose which bits are needed. That's what we have tried to do as a result of the National Curriculum review. We have slimmed it down, made it more flexible and less detailed, and we have tried to define, through consultation, the rationale for each of the subjects.

I'm really excited about the next version of the National Curriculum. We are producing it with pictures, quotes from famous people, examples of children's work, which makes it clear (for example) why D & T is important as a subject, why mathematics is important, why English is important, and so on. It's printed in multicolour – with pupils' work, with quotes from people from the Royal Society, quotes from famous athletes, and such like, saying what really turned them on. We have spent two and a half years working on this, in terms of conveying the excitement of the curriculum and why we do things. It stresses children's learning and children's perception of the importance of this today. It's going to have a big impact.

**R.C.W.** Assuming the technicolour vision transfers to the classroom?

**N.T.** Of course, we then need to convert this vision into reality, through teachers looking at how they teach and how they enable children to learn. There is a long way to go in terms of moving to approaches that are going to get children engaged, are going to give them a sense of why they are doing it and how it relates to them. Our schools (especially secondary schools) are full of children – some of whom are very bright – who are bored out of their minds and who haven't a clue why they are being asked to do things. They don't want to be in a place where there is virtually no engagement between their passions and the world of learning. That's why, whilst I'm not one of these deschoolers who would dismantle the curriculum and transform everything into interdisciplinary projects, I am interested to explore what we can do to make the curriculum more engaging. Which is one reason why we commissioned the Demos Report, *The Creative Age* (Bentley and Seltzer 1999a), which offers some very radical thoughts on curriculum structures and content.

In any discussion about interdisciplinary studies, there is a danger that the rigour of subject disciplines could get lost. Some of the best post-16 teaching I've seen has been on a very traditional A level history syllabus, where the teacher really had an understanding of why, for two years, young people of that age should be doing history. Whilst he knew he was teaching history, he was also aware that he was helping young people to interact, to plan their learning, to investigate and all the rest of it. He had a vision of what he was enabling those children to do. There was so much more than enabling the young people to get good grades (which they did). The curriculum, the syllabus, the exam were all used brilliantly as a vehicle for all these other things. That's a lot to do with having a clear concept of what education is all about.

**R.C.W.** Is it also about giving teachers more freedom in terms of how they interpret the set of objectives relating to a subject such as history?

**N.T.** It's a case of chicken and egg. There are a few teachers I would be terrified to leave to choose the material, quite honestly. The important issue is the quality of work.

**R.C.W.** You talked earlier about GCSE results, and of course these do drive schools and teachers to eliminate or ignore some materials. Do the assessment structures exert too much influence on what is taught?

**N.T.** This is one of the rather interesting themes that did emerge out of this year's results. There was a very good editorial in the *TES* in the summer (*TES* editorial 1999), arguing that we are over-assessed in this country, compared to other parts of Europe. On occasions I have said that we might need to ask questions about the long-term future of GCSE. We have been given a commission to look at 14–19 coherence, which is very welcome because we can begin to not just ask the questions, but also come up with some possible answers to them. But no other country in the world has the panacea to these problems either.

**R.C.W.** The RSA report *Opening Minds* (Bayliss 1999) echoes your point that there should be more clarity about what students need to learn – and the purpose education should serve. What's your reaction to its proposal that the curriculum should be competence-led rather than information-led, with subjects as illustrative material rather than the end in itself?

**N.T.** I think there's a matrix here that's very important. But I think the RSA document goes too far, as does the Demos report on creativity. It's rather similar to the theme of Ken Robinson's report about creativity, culture and education (DfEE 1999e). In all these examples it seems to me there's an element of over-reaction, which perpetuates the knowledge versus skills battleground. I think that there are certain bits of knowledge – whether scientific, technological, cultural, historical or whatever – that you are really disadvantaged and deprived if you don't have. You actually lose a frame of reference, which enables subsequent creativity and is a launchpad for all sorts of other things, if schools do not provide it.

So you have to strike a balance between the Demos suggestion that we dramatically cut masses of content out of the National Curriculum and the kinds of programmes of study that the French still have. In France the curriculum is exhaustively detailed, and they are desperately trying to cut back on the prescriptive detail. There has to be a middle path, and that's what we have been trying to create with the revisions of the National Curriculum. We live in a society which does rather downplay cultural knowledge at the expense of transferable skills. There is a problem here, though. For instance, I interview a lot of people who have the most splendid communication and social skills, but have very little to communicate. There isn't much in their minds. These are people who have all the interpersonal skills and are immensely employable in that sense – but there's nowt there. One of the things that has to be there before anything else can be there is a huge store of knowledge and references, and some intelligent connections between these things.

**R.C.W.** The RSA view and the Demos view is that these changes are necessary to prepare children effectively for adult life in the twenty-first century, and to ensure that our own culture and society flourishes and prospers. Do you think the curriculum has the potential to be more of a glue for a cohesive society?

**N.T.** Oh yes, I feel very strongly about that. This is one of the strengths of the French system. One of the huge advantages of the National Curriculum and why we shouldn't get rid of it, even if we pare it down, is that it does provide a common grounding for all children and a common introduction to their world, to their society. It gives them a common set of references. In a global society where differences between cultures are being diminished, for all sorts of reasons, I think it's terribly important that people have a sense of belonging. I would like independent schools to choose to follow it for this reason and many of them do – especially in the lead up to GCSEs when it's actually rather sensible to follow the National Curriculum. I do worry about disapplying the National Curriculum to certain groups in certain schools and the extent to which people say, 'Well, you don't have to do the National Curriculum in Educational Action Zones.' I think it provides cultural and social cement, which is very important.

**R.C.W.** Thank you.

# 12

# Interview with Professor Ted Wragg

School of Education, University of Exeter

**Roger Crombie White**  Can I start with your early experiences of school?

**Ted Wragg**  I went to a very mixed primary school in Sheffield, which was right on the borderline between a working-class and a lower middle-class area, with a more middle-class area further away. Because it was on a tram route, it took people from a mile up and down the road. So it actually recruited people from all kinds of backgrounds.

**R.C.W.**  Did you enjoy it?

**T.W.**  I didn't like Infants. I remember my first day well. I sat next to somebody who was threading beads onto a piece of cotton, and I thought, 'If this is school, count me out.' But I liked learning to read and write, I thought that was great. The *Beacon Readers* were OK, although I never could understand all these daddies who dug gardens. If you lived in working-class Sheffield and your dad was in the steelworks, as mine was, you didn't come home and dig up the concrete backyard. There was no garden within probably about half a mile of where I lived.

**R.C.W.**  Was the secondary school the same sort of mix?

**T.W.**  No, the secondary school was different because it was the most academic grammar school in Sheffield. At that time, with the 11-plus, Sheffield schools were finely graded. The top 120 boys went to King Edward's, and the top 120 girls went to the Girls' High School. I had what was called an Ecclesall Bierlow scholarship, which was the princely sum of £6, paid in three instalments in your first three years.

**R.C.W.**  £6 a year?

**T.W.**  No! £6 in all – £1.10.0, then £3, then £1.10.0. Something quaint about that. Nowadays it wouldn't even buy you a Coca-Cola.

**R.C.W.**  Presumably you enjoyed that too if it wasn't threading beads?

**T.W.**  I had 20 lessons a week of grammar, because I did Latin, English, French and German. So I'm actually red-hot on grammar. I like grammar.

There were lots of good things, but what was defective were some of the teaching methods, which I thought were very dreary. There was an enormous amount of clock-watching. But I enjoyed it mostly. The other thing it was very good for was extra-curricular activities. I acted in a number of school plays, and for years afterwards I knew plays like Julius Caesar off by heart because I'd played Brutus.

Funnily enough, a few weeks ago I watched the black and white Marlon Brando film of Julius Caesar. Brando's Mark Anthony speech is just a stunning piece of theatre. And I'm just so glad that we could actually act Shakespeare.

**R.C.W.** Looking back, are there things that you wish you'd experienced, but didn't?

**T.W.** I wish I'd had better art teaching because I'm useless at art. I didn't like it at school, although I do like art now thanks to one of my own PGCE students, who was a very talented artist himself and one of our best art teachers in that particular year. He got all of our mixed tutorial group painting, and it was a complete eye-opener, what art was really about. Most of us did the best drawings and the best paintings we'd ever done in our lives, because this bloke actually taught us how to draw and paint in just one or two sessions.

I didn't like geography either. I blame some really dreary teaching, which reduced what should have been extremely exciting stuff to arrows and symbols on maps that nobody was the slightest bit interested in.

**R.C.W.** Thinking back to the Teacher Training Agency ad, 'No-one forgets a good teacher', were there particular teachers that linger in your memory?

**T.W.** One that I've often quoted is the teacher who took us in Junior 3 and 4 at the primary school (because we had the same teacher for two years) – a man called George Long, who went on to be Chief Primary Adviser in Sheffield. He was way ahead of his time in terms of what he got us to do. He had us involved with some terrific projects which, when everything was 11-plus mad, was very unusual. I did projects about the history of flight, the history of medicine, cocoa, and such like. To learn about Pasteur for instance, I taught myself. George didn't have a clue himself about the history of medicine. But I went to the library and read about Pasteur and Lister. The same with the history of flight, which he didn't know much about. But I found out all about the Montgolfier Brothers and Alcock and Brown and the Wright Brothers and so on. The R101 . . .

**R.C.W.** Although he didn't know much about it himself you describe him as a good teacher?

**T.W.** It was early topic and project work. Whenever I talk about a curriculum for the twenty-first century, and about the importance of content and process, I often give this example of being taken down to Sheffield reference library by George Long when I was 10, and being shown how to find out information in the reference library.

**R.C.W.** The Dewey system you mean?

**T.W.** Yes, what bibliographies were, what encyclopedias were and so on. Not only do I remember the content, I actually remember the process. What's more, years afterwards, when I was back home on university vacations, or when I was doing my Masters and my PhD, I occasionally went in that library and I met people that I'd known at primary school. And we'd talk about George.

Another bloke was the man who taught music in the grammar school who had no discipline whatsoever. He broke all the stereotypes in the sense that, if you had watched his lessons, you would have probably said they were rowdy. Yet, every time I meet people from my school they immediately start talking about music. There is a huge number of kids who've got a lifelong interest in music because of this one man.

**R.C.W.** Despite the rowdiness?

**T.W.** It was good-natured rowdiness. If we were going to sing or do something, we'd stop. The rowdiness was part of the excitement really. I was interested in music anyway, because I come from a musical family. But the stuff I learnt from him is still with me now. Recently I went to the Bournemouth Symphony Orchestra and heard Haydn's London Symphony, which I did for O level. I knew every note in that symphony. I hadn't heard it for some time but I kept thinking, 'Ah, that phrase is slightly different from the normal one, because it's the last time it occurs, and it's in a transitional part of the symphony.' It all came back to me.

**R.C.W.** Having gone to university and trained as a teacher you then taught in a grammar school. Yet in your writing now, you're very critical of the grammar school/secondary modern system. Why is this?

**T.W.** I started teaching in Wakefield in the sixties, when it was assumed that graduates went into grammar schools. I enjoyed it; I thought they were fun places to be, lots of bright kids, lots you could do. But I was well aware it was a highly divided system, so I volunteered to go and teach other kinds of kids because I didn't want to just teach the brightest. The city had a youth exchange with German and French towns, and I volunteered to teach everyone who went over from Wakefield schools to Germany. Most of them were secondary modern kids and didn't know a single word of German. They were to go in the summer, and I started in September. I taught them for two hours on a Tuesday night to try and get them up to a reasonable standard of conversational German. I loved every second of that because here were kids who'd never had a chance.

There was one lad who was a miner. He was 16 and he was already down the mine, because he had left school at 15. Remember this was the sixties. Usually he'd had a quick shower, but sometimes he just had to grab his kit and rush off to my class. He'd come in with the pit grime still on him. When the German youth group were in Wakefield for the reciprocal leg of the exchange I remember he actually made a speech in German, thanking them for their hospitality. That was a secondary modern school lad who'd gone down the pit. He showed me a draft of his speech – it was full of minor grammatical errors and grossly misspelt, but orally he was fluent.

I met so many boys and girls like him who had never had a chance. That was my first taste of teaching right across the ability range and I felt an enormous sense of injustice. Here were all these capable people, when CSE was just coming in, who were leaving with not a single piece of paper to recognize anything they'd done at school. 80 per cent of the population.

I've always opposed the return of selection. Now we've got a third of kids going to higher education, and their equivalent grandparents – and many of their equivalent parents – would never have even got one graded certificate for anything. It's absolutely ludicrous that it took so long to change. This third leave with a degree – even if it's not a brilliant degree in some cases – and their grandparents left with nothing, and their parents left with half a dozen CSEs. Yet they are all of similar ability. I think that's the triumph of education.

**R.C.W.**  Yet there's another two-thirds who don't go on after school.

**T.W.**  Yes, but now there are 46 per cent of the population getting five high-grade GCSEs, compared with 20 per cent only a few years ago. So you've got another batch of kids who are leaving with quite a nice portfolio of exam results. And instead of 80 per cent leaving with absolutely nothing, it's down to 7 per cent. There are still problems, but it seems to me they are of a different order.

**R.C.W.**  So when you mentioned a curriculum for the twenty-first century, would your view be that there is just a bit of tweaking to be done? To tap away at that 7 per cent who aren't succeeding? Or is there something more dramatic?

**T.W.**  There's a set of issues that need addressing, one of which concerns the 7 per cent leaving with nothing. Some of these are people with severe learning difficulties; some may come from a very difficult background. It may not be necessary for them to get GCSEs, but many of them are at risk in a society where there's frankly not much time for the vulnerable.

Another issue is the relatively low achievement of boys. Many boys are not able to walk straight out into lorry loading and muscular jobs, because forklift trucks are doing all that now. A lot of the jobs on offer involve communications and they are not always terribly good at that. I think that's one of the biggest challenges facing us. Otherwise we could have a largish group of disaffected people, who know they've got potential, but somehow were never able to realize it, for whatever reason. So it may well come out in antisocial forms.

**R.C.W.** Is this a curriculum issue?

**T.W.** It's the way in which the curriculum is addressed, as much as what is in it. I like Roland Meighan's idea of the curriculum being seen to some extent as a shopping catalogue, where you can get things from your teachers, or from your parents, or your friends. Or you may dig them out yourself, using appropriate technology.

**R.C.W.** Is this an argument for deschooling?

**T.W.** It would be if you take it to an extreme, but I think it's just a question of options. If 90 per cent of children are quite happily going to schools, getting a fair amount out of it, and 10 per cent are doing other things, then it's not really deschooling. I think it would be catastrophic if we deschooled – an absolute disaster. I wouldn't touch it with four barge poles tied together. But for certain kids, yes.

I saw some very interesting work in a school in Brooklyn where they'd tried everything to get kids off the streets. These were kids who were at the mercy of drug dealers and street thieves. Some were killed. So they tried lots of programmes; they even took education out to disused warehouses and corner cafes. And of course then they ran into problems because some of the students who were turning up for everyday lessons said, 'We turn up for everyday lessons and get the standard menu. These people stay away and you take the education to them, you do what they want. It isn't fair.'

The story that best illustrates the dilemma is the one about two people walking along the beach where all these starfish are twitching and dying as the water is going out. One keeps lobbing a few back into the water until his companion says, 'What's the point of that? There are thousands of them twitching and dying on the sand. It's pretty pointless just lobbing in one or two.' But his friend picks up another couple, throws them in and says, 'Yes, it's not pointless for them though.'

**R.C.W.** So that's two issues – boys' under-achievement and the tail-enders. What about resources? Many of the young people interviewed here make comparisons with their friends who are in independent schools. Is that something we're just going to have to live with?

**T.W.** Of course the resourcing of education is an issue. Having been to places like City Technology Colleges and seen how well kitted-out they are, and then going to a school where there is a queue for the two computers in the classroom, that's clearly unfair. It's interesting to look at the Scandinavian countries, which have a much better sense of universal social justice than we have. In Norway, for example, there's an overwhelmingly strong feeling about entitlement and the children of the Lapps are entitled to have just as square a deal as the children of Oslo. And if they didn't there would be uproar.

However, all the time I've worked in education we've had the Victorian railway carriage system in this country. Whether it's grammars and secondary moderns and all-age schools, or whether it's uptown and down-town, or whether it's private and maintained, or our current three-tier system of private, semi-private (i.e. grant maintained and City Techno-logy Colleges) and then the rest. We've had it, one way or another, all along, and there's a sort of fatalism about it almost, as if humanity is designed to be divided into three groups, whether you call them gold, silver and bronze, or first-class, second-class and third-class, or whatever. That's the way it is and isn't it rotten? And that's where I feel more could be done. Which is why I welcome Education Action Zones and why I was sorry that social priority schools and educational priority areas ever disappeared in the first place.

**R.C.W.**  But some would say this tiered system is OK, because eventually the third-class schools will close and the first-class ones will expand . . .

**T.W.**  The idea that the market place takes care of quality by itself is one of the most bogus arguments that ever emerged from the Thatcher years. The tragic example that gives the lie to that is the Lyme Bay tragedy (Young 1993). Four children died because they went to a substandard field centre. Of course the market place did control quality, because it was shut down. So you could argue that the market does help things find their level eventually, which matters not one jot if some spigot manufac-turer goes bust because his product's lousy and his shareholders weren't interested, but it does matter if someone's life goes bust. It's interesting that in the United States, the land of the free, you have the most rigorous control of field centres. Many states have adopted New York's very stiff criteria for becoming an accredited private field centre because it gives an assurance to parents and teachers that these camps and field centres and so on are safe for their kids to go to. There you've got a very good example of a free market with a degree of regulation built in.

**R.C.W.**  But how do you apply that to schools? You talk about social justice, but there is a huge disparity between certain schools.

**T.W.**  Our only option for the twenty-first century is to make every school a good school. What the Conservatives called parental choice was choice for a smallish number of parents to send their kids to a grammar school. Or for the more vocal and more powerful to be able to send their child to a school outside their own area. There was no choice for people who didn't pass an 11-plus or people whose parents were scared of authority, or who didn't speak English. They got what was left.

I would want to encourage the many schools that are doing well to carry on doing well and to improve. A fair number of schools could do better and they should be supported to do better. Some schools are not doing at all well and radical steps should be taken to improve what they are doing. It sounds like Ofsted, but the difference lies with the methods and the climate. With Ofsted it's more pressure than support. I'd want to see much more support and less pressure.

I'm in favour of inspection but I'm strongly opposed to the form that we've actually got. When Tim Brighouse and I wrote our paper about a better model of inspection, we called it 'a better model of inspection', not 'no model of inspection'. One or two Ofsted spokespeople have tried to make out that anybody who is against Ofsted is against inspection. It's not true. Very few people are against inspection, but large numbers of people don't like Ofsted.

What matters is genuine, quality education for all and no stone should be left unturned. If there is a school that is doing badly, every effort should be made to turn it round, including closing it if all else fails.

**R.C.W.** But a lot of the debate hinges on what counts as quality . . .

**T.W.** When the history of education in the twentieth century is written, with a bit of objectivity in 2020, people will throw up their hands in horror, as we've tended to do about payment by results. How did it happen that quality became equated with bureaucracy? I mean, why are hospital consultants now spending five hours a week more on bureaucracy and two hours a week less with patients? Because quality assurance is actually seen as committees, working groups, form filling and structures. I don't know how true this is but someone told me that some school that had been given an A for its quality assurance had actually failed its inspection. That's so laughable. Like Lenny Bruce said about Kissinger getting the Nobel Prize, 'Satire is now officially dead.' Satire can't compete with this stuff, real life wins hands down.

**R.C.W.** So what counts as quality, in your view?

**T.W.** It's bespoke. My objection is to treating 24,000 schools or 400,000 teachers or eight million children as if they are all the same, as if there's a national standard for sausages and they are just measured against that. It's so monumentally crude. Why weren't the people proposing it run out of town? All this stuff about prescribing teaching methods. This is for people who are so hopeless that they don't know what they are doing and need to be told exactly what to do so that they don't injure somebody. But people who know what they are doing should be supported.

The current shibboleth is the statement, 'There is no point in finding different solutions to common problems.' It's said by Ofsted, the Teacher Training Agency, and politicians. It's completely bogus. What you are really saying is, 'There is only one solution.' If there are two, then there is no point in looking for more than one solution. If there is no point, then there is just one solution. What's the one solution? Who knows? The one solution is whatever the most powerful people of the day impose, not the best solution.

What's the single solution to poverty? What's the single solution to crime? Or world conflict? The environment? Cancer? Where are these single solutions to common problems? However, in education current orthodoxy has a single solution that should be wished on people. Yet any notion that eight million kids need a standard procedure is just so laughable it shouldn't even have been given one sentence of time.

**R.C.W.** Come 2020 – what striking differences would you want to see?

**T.W.** A huge investment in people at all levels, rather than in systems. Systems will need to be there to facilitate what people actually do – so they don't duplicate each other or waste time unnecessarily, so they can communicate with each other. But within that both teachers and pupils are encouraged to find solutions. And these solutions might be different from each other – within the same class, within different classes in the same school, within the same local authorities.

**R.C.W.** You'd be against comparisons between schools?

**T.W.** Crude comparisons, yes. Friendly comparisons for information. The sort of comparison I like is when I go to a school and say, 'I was in a school like yours and they ran a book club.' And someone will say, 'But it wouldn't work in our school.' And I say, 'Well actually, if anything, the two schools are pretty similar in terms of their intake.'

I would scrap league tables in any form. I'm in favour of parents having information, but not in league tables. I think the mischief done by league tables is far greater than any mischief that might be done by giving people information about one school but not necessarily about others miles away. I was never in favour of schools having reading tests scored and not disclosing them. If parents want to know, they should have the right to know. But that's not the same as league tables.

I'm not in favour of value-added league tables either, because you get new artefacts. There was a lot of propaganda last year about cruising schools, much of it coming from Ofsted. The idea was that you would look at test scores aged 14 and compare them with GCSEs. A simple formula was worked out to give a school an A, B, C, D or E. The interesting thing was some of the most highly respected schools in the country got a D or an E (including Ofsted Beacon schools). The results were never published and that was simply because these schools would have been made to look as if they were cruising. If it had been some downtown comprehensive school, the press, politicians, Ofsted – everybody – would have said they had been rumbled. However, because it was highly selective schools in some cases, people said, 'Well, that can't be right. It's an artefact. Therefore we're not having it.'

**R.C.W.** What else would you want to see in 2020?

**T.W.** The exciting thing about education is an unrequited quest for solution. Finding best solutions in different circumstances is really what professional expertise is about. Sometimes best solutions are doing things with individuals or small groups; sometimes best solutions are whole-class teaching. I tell stories to 5-year-olds sometimes, but I'm not going to tell them all individually. If I can't hold the attention of thirty kids telling them a story, I'll hang my boots up.

There's a mixture of solutions which are feasible. They are not pie in the sky. And they are not going to be universal. But they are worth searching for. That's where the joy has gone out of teaching for a lot of people. The more that was imposed, the more they felt that their fundamental professional right to seek best solutions was being thwarted.

I could feel very optimistic about the future, if people are trusted. Right now we've got this high-accountability, low-trust system. If there were one thing I would do for the twenty-first century, I'd reverse it, like a seesaw. I'd just tilt it the other way and go for high trust, low accountability. About seven-eighths of a seesaw swings.

**R.C.W.** Trust the teachers.

**T.W.** With 400,000 teachers, you know that some will let you down. There's no point in being foolishly optimistic. Some will betray your trust, but I think we want a massive liberation of expectations and much more trust. Last night there was a programme about this guru in America, who charges forty thousand a day to sort out organizational problems. He was asked what was critical and he said, 'Trust people.' At £20,000 a word, it's probably cheap at the price if it actually makes an impact.

**R.C.W.** That's a good note to end on: 'Trust people.' Thanks very much.

# 13

# Values and vision: social justice

'The world is in such an awful state,
When I'm older I'll make it great.
No more wars or pollution
How I wish I could find a solution.
No more oil in the sea.
But this won't happen just because of me.
So I'll find some people to help me,
and together, we'll save the
WORLD!'
                    Tamsin Elliott, age 8, in *Our World 2000* (Save the Children 1999)

There is a lot in what the young people say in the earlier chapters of this book, which finds echoes in the comments by the adult interviewees.

The young people value process-based education; they want professional teachers; they stress the importance of relationships within the school – both with teachers and their friends; they want decent resources; they have some deep-seated concerns about the state of society. And the adults share these concerns. They want curriculum reform, structural reform and, perhaps most importantly, they want attitudinal reform – a shift in the way education is perceived and supported.

The devil is not (as is commonly said) in the detail. One of the problems we are facing is that we often allow the focus with regard to educational reform to be on the detail of the map at the expense of the territory itself. We concentrate on changing some of the symbols, realigning a few contours, upgrading a few roads, while ignoring the world that the map represents. For instance, curriculum issues have been at the forefront of educational debate for the past three decades, pushing aside many other issues that may well be even more important for all of us, such as the combined impact of league tables, parental choice and open enrolment on '*secondary* modernizing the comprehensive principle' (to slightly misquote Tony Blair). Alongside what is happening in the housing market, where we are witnessing rapidly expanding differentials in prices between the desirable and not so desirable areas of our towns and cities, these factors create a situation where the rich and poor are more segregated than they've ever been. As Will Hutton wrote in an article in the *Observer*, headlined 'The real cost of the property boom':

> This makes any attempt at constructing socially balanced communities impossible, and undercuts the principle of comprehensive education . . . A new housing apartheid is emerging, creating a social laager for the new superclass who are migrating from the rest of the country to live in the streets and the districts where they can find others as rich as themselves.
>
> (Hutton 1999)

Very few urban secondary schools are now really comprehensive in anything but name, because catchment areas contain increasingly polarized communities in terms of wealth and culture, and those parents with enough resources can usually succeed in moving house or leapfrogging catchment boundaries to get their children into the 'popular' schools. Some parents are not above fabricating addresses in sought-after areas, or renting small flats for a short period simply to secure a postal address from which to claim legitimate access to a desirable school (Bright 1999).

This segregation is compounded, of course, by the existence of private schools, which have always offered an alternative to the state sector for parents with sufficient wealth. Although many private schools offer generous bursaries and scholarships to those with ability from poorer homes (reflecting in many cases the purposes for which they were originally endowed), it is inevitable that their intake will be weighted towards particular social class groupings, which is precisely why many parents choose them in the first place. In some cities the private sector caters for a high percentage of secondary age children. In Bristol, for instance, 23 per cent of 11-year-olds either attend private schools or travel outside the LEA at the point of transition to secondary school, which is bound to have an impact on the overall levels of attainment at the local comprehensive.

Any analysis of educational provision must include the private sector as well as the state sector. We need to be clear about how the overall structure of the educational system in the UK at the beginning of the twenty-first century impacts on the *whole* population in terms of the way it opens doors to wealth and health and privilege and rewarding work. Is it effective? Is it fair? Is it a system that we wish to sustain? Right at the heart of all this is an even more important question about what kind of society we want to live in and want our children and grandchildren to inherit. The structure of this will be shaped by the values that we hold to be most important, and will be reflected in, and reinforced by, the form and content of our system of education.

This is simply the most important national purpose for us, in the first few years of the twenty-first century: to raise our education standards significantly . . . For every school that is not functioning as well as it could do, for every child that is deprived of an education, that is a huge injustice. They are not getting the start in life they need . . . If we don't have a first class, well educated workforce, then we can't compete. It is the single biggest driver of increased productivity.

> (Tony Blair quoted in an interview with
> Caroline St. John-Brooks 21 January 2000)

The Prime Minister is optimistic that, given time, we can overcome the stark differences of income and social class which have made the UK one of the most polarized societies in the developed world.

The whole purpose of what we're doing is to raise up the standards within the system, so that children, even if they are from poor family backgrounds and living in inner cities where there's not much opportunity around, get the chance through decent education to do well . . . The idea of comprehensive education was to get away from dividing up kids as successes and failures at the age of 11 and splitting them up in this very rigid way – 20 per cent successes and 80 per cent ending up in the second division of education. What people must switch from is thinking that comprehensive means 'one size fits all'. Whereas it's about making sure that you have the full range of abilities catered for within the system.

> (Tony Blair 21 January 2000)

It is very interesting to contrast Tony Blair's vision of an inclusive education system with one of Margaret Thatcher's most quoted remarks in the 1980s, 'There is no such thing as society.' Although this was contradicted slightly by her successor John Major, in the wake of the Jamie Bulger murder, with his poetic aphorism, 'Society must condemn a little more and understand a little less', the philosophy that underpinned both these statements was one that emphasized the importance of the individual as a lone operator – striking out against 'socialist' tendencies that would merely reduce everyone to the lowest common denominator. 'Me first' was to be encouraged, because (the argument went) if the rich were enabled to get richer, this would trickle down to the poorer members of society. Everyone would benefit.

Yet, as the Joseph Rowntree report (Hills 1998) of wealth distribution showed, the gap between the rich and the poor widened considerably during the 18 years the Conservative Party were in power from 1979 to 1997. Salaries for senior executives rocketed to scandalous heights, except that it was not even acknowledged to be scandalous. When the chief executive of Railtrack was interviewed on Newsnight at the time of the Paddington rail crash in October 1999, Kirsty Wark pointed out that his salary was £430,000. He saw nothing wrong with this; nor indeed did the whole echelon of senior managers in receipt of similarly inflated payments.

It was all a product of the free market, where 'market forces' would determine outcomes. The strong and successful would simply attract more shareholders' funding and go on to be even more successful. The weak and ineffective would go to the wall. The removal of regulation in relation to public services would liberate competitive forces for everyone's benefit. Standards could only improve. The privatization of public services would encourage even more successful practice. Local authority services, public utilities, national and regional transport, and schools were set free in the market to float free of straitjacketed systems. Things would find their own level, and the outcome would be an improvement in quality.

As Ted Wragg says (p. 135), the lie to this in educational terms was the Lyme Bay tragedy (in which four young canoeists died), where an unregulated market had no control over its operators. Finally, the market place did intervene, because the field centre was closed down, but only after four lives had been lost. Ted Wragg points to the countless other lives that have 'gone bust' in an educational system that judges success by the narrowest and most unfairly demarcated set of indicators, which take no account whatsoever of the starting point of a school. 'You can fool some of the people all of the time, and all of the people some of the time, but you can't fool all of the people all of the time.' However, with the annual ritual of the publication of league table results, it seems we have come pretty close to achieving this ultimate state of being universally hoodwinked. The hallowed stature accorded to league tables by the media has resonances with the story of the Emperor's clothes. 'Satire is officially dead. Real life wins hands down,' concludes Ted Wragg.

What is remarkable in England and Wales is that only a handful of voices are seriously challenging the reification of league tables and performance 'targets' (Moore 1999; Cohen 2000; Wragg 2000), even though anyone who thinks about it for more than a few seconds knows that the overall output at 16 depends so much on the quality of the intake at 11. Of course schools can make a difference and a good school can make a lot of difference. But what matters even more is the ability of the children when they enter the school.

In 1998, when the DfEE proposed extending its evaluation of coasting schools to the 166 grammar schools, this was a welcome ray of light. GCSE scores would be compared against Key Stage 2 attainment targets to identify the 'added value' of the school. The important figure would be the difference between the predicted results and the actual performance, given the ability of the intake. Clearly, with this yardstick, schools which traditionally appeared at the top of the league tables might fare less well in a value-added comparison. Some selective schools achieving 70 per cent or 80 per cent may actually be shown to be less effective than schools with 30 per cent or 40 per cent, which would be a significant boost to those arguing that judgements being made about good or bad schools on the basis of raw

GCSE results were fundamentally flawed (White 1999a, 1999b). This would make a huge difference to those many comprehensives which succeed in raising achievement levels of all their pupils way beyond normal expectations (including those pupils whose performance will never enhance league table comparisons), yet are frequently overlooked by parents for whom the raw score is all that matters. Interestingly, the results of this evaluation have yet to be published, even though a *TES* analysis showed that a number of grammar schools fell well below government expectations (Dean and Rafferty 1998) and research by Professor David Jesson at York University revealed that more able students actually performed better in comprehensive schools (Dean 1999; Barnard 2000).

On top of this, and quite apart from ability of intake, there are other factors that are equally significant when making comparative judgements about the achievement of schools. Although they will certainly share a common curriculum and most likely have a comparable spread of good teachers, their resource base of equipment, teaching rooms and the involvement of parents may differ widely. These differentials can often be exacerbated as time goes by for the reasons outlined already. If the more affluent parents gravitate towards particular schools, the school can reckon on a rising level of support for its own fundraising activities, alongside diminishing expenditure on the costs of mitigating disadvantage among its pupils. Certain children can be more costly to educate and, if there are less of these in the school, there is a saving all round from which everyone else benefits. If there are more around, it can be wearing on staff time, resources and the fabric of the building. Those schools who take a disproportionate number of pupils with emotional and behavioural problems know this only too well.

This situation has been exacerbated by the free market approach to education adopted by the Conservative government in the 1980s and 1990s. Open enrolment combined with parental choice has dramatically altered the social class intake of many schools. In an interview for *The Guardian* in September 1999, Kenneth Baker revealed some of the manipulative thinking behind the 1988 Act.

> I legislated for LMS and it diminished the power of the LEAs and the teacher unions. Certainly there was a political edge to the attack on LEAs, but then they had a political agenda too. I wanted them to wither on the vine. I would have liked to bring back selection but I would have got into such controversy. I hoped choice would open it all up and it would lead to the poorer schools having to close.
>
> (Davies 1999)

The Conservatives have made no secret of the political motives that lay behind their educational reforms and the value base that underpinned them. David Blunkett's inheritance was designed and developed by those who believed in selection, and in using the education system to preserve existing hierarchies. It seemed to be of little concern if young people left school illiterate or unemployed, except in so far as they might pose a threat to social order.

Now, with a Labour government, it is possible to see a rather different set of values in the ascendancy. There is a commitment to the state sector that has not been seen for twenty years. Chapter 6 made reference to *Excellence in Cities* (DfEE 1999a) and, although it is still early days, the evidence is that things are changing. Certainly funding is being made available to address some of the inequalities that exist in society, as confirmed by respective government annual reports (HMSO 1999). Alongside the educational changes, we have New Deal, which has already achieved phenomenal results, cutting the number of young people who had been jobless for more than a year from 62,000 to 9200 in just two years – an 85 per cent drop (Toynbee 1999), although critics have expressed concern about the permanence of many of these jobs (Slater 2000).

In the interview for the *TES* quoted on page 141, Tony Blair refers to the 'huge injustice' of having a system where some children are deprived of an effective education, and the phrase 'social justice' is an oft-repeated refrain by the adults interviewed here. It is clearly something that matters to them all and it may be interesting to reflect on this further.

How is it that people like Anita Higham, Ted Wragg, Richard Pring, Tim Brighouse, Nick Tate and David Blunkett have given their working lives to 'public service', earning substantially less money than they might have earned in the private sector? Of course none of them are 'poor', but the salary of a university professor, chief education officer, head teacher, chief executive of QCA, or even the Secretary of State for Education are not in the same league as the chief executive of Railtrack or the bosses of any of the other privatized utilities. What drew these 'successful' products of our grammar school system back into the world of state education? The stories they tell in this book provide some intriguing insights into the interplay of chance and design, and how they have acquired a commitment to a particular set of values.

We have a unique opportunity. As Richard Pring says, 'For the first time in our history we have a Prime Minister, Permanent Secretary and Secretary of State for Education who send their children to the state system.' Although critics point out that the London Oratory represents the more richly resourced end of the state-supported spectrum (Thornton 1999), there is, nevertheless, a genuine awareness in the corridors of power of the experience that ordinary children are going through, and the pressures and constraints on teachers, schools and local education authorities. On page 92 David Blunkett talks about his own choices as a parent of three teenage boys.

I felt a real obligation to work to make the system better ... which is what I tried to do. It's difficult to talk about this because I don't want to condemn parents who have taken a different view. Each of us make a judgement according to very different circumstances.

Ted Wragg, Richard Pring and Tim Brighouse also chose to put their children through the state system for very positive reasons.

> The city we lived in when the children were at secondary school had a comprehensive system. We bought a house and the local school was the wrong side of the tracks. But I knew it was a very good school . . . Academically mine did OK. Both of them came out with first-class honours degrees. Both of them have got a range of friends and understandings that I didn't have because they went to a comprehensive school.
>
> (Brighouse, page 102)

> My children experienced a quality to learning that they would not have received had they gone to a private system. They came across teachers who were exceedingly good, very dedicated, very caring, and they came to appreciate working and learning to live with children who came from disadvantaged homes . . . Those comprehensive schools that they went to in the formative parts of their lives have been very successful. One of the great sadnesses though is that a lot of their friends at primary school disappeared off to private schools, reinforcing this socially divided society, which we have, and which continues to be reinforced by a select, private system of schooling.
>
> (Pring, page 118)

The whole issue of the extent to which the private and public sectors of education can mutually coexist is a critical one for discussion. The choices facing parents of primary school children at the start of Year 6 can be excruciating, as some parents forsake the local comprehensive in favour of schools further away or in the private sector. Judgements made about individual choices can become quite embittered. The kind of tolerance evidenced by David Blunkett's remark above is not always the common experience.

However, at the same time as respecting the rights of parents to make individual choices for their own children, we need to examine the impact of such choices on other people's children.

> There's always a huge dichotomy between dealing with the needs of an individual and the needs of the wider society. When you are dealing with an individual couple of parents all you can say is, 'You must do what you believe is in the best interests of your own child.' When you are looking at the needs of a whole nation or a local authority area though, and you're looking at a timespan of ten, twenty, thirty years hence, you have to look at it somewhat differently. It's very complex.
>
> (Higham, page 112)

Some of the sixth formers from state schools put it very well.

'Because the private schools can hand pick their students, they're bound to get better grades, and then get more funding. If I was David Blunkett I'd direct where the money is going so that some schools get more than others. It isn't fair that some schools have fantastic facilities, like sports halls, swimming pools, tennis courts, or masses of computers, whilst others have very little.'

(Jonathan, p. 57)

'You can't deny people the choice to send their children to private schools, but on the other hand you shouldn't deny other people the opportunity to go there too. There's a massive conflict here. If I was Secretary of State I'd force them to share with the state system, so that every school can be a good school.'

(Mike C., p. 58)

The response from some of those in the independent sector is equally well argued.

'If you've got a lot of money and you want to buy a BMW instead of a Ford escort, that's an option that's available. If you've got the money and you feel that you should send your child to one of these schools then it's an option that's there for you.'

(Alex M., p. 59)

'The problem with phasing out the assisted places scheme is that those children whose parents aren't so well off can't have an equal chance.'

(Joshua, p. 59)

'You talked about trying to make ordinary schools better, but that might be a waste of money because a lot of people don't want to learn. I'm not saying, 'Don't give them an education,' but if you do want to bring up standards in education, you need to have a few schools that are better and people who want to go to them. Quite a few kids don't. They don't see education as a major thing in their lives.'

(Nawaz, p. 59)

In opening up the debate about private and public schooling, I am aware that feelings can run very high, but that is not a reason for avoiding the exploration. When Anita Higham uses the phrase 'educational apartheid' to describe the current situation, she acknowledges the emotive force of such words, but believes it to be an accurate description of the interplay between public and private schooling and between different schools within each sector. The 'separate development' of children from (mostly) wealthy, professional backgrounds in richly resourced schools, well away from the influences of those from less affluent or less motivated homes, contributes to the maintenance of a divided and hierarchical society.

This is not an exhortation to rise up and storm the barricades of privilege and destroy the very edifice of our 'public' schools, although we should note that the Labour Party Conference of 1981 committed itself, by a majority of seven million to seven thousand, to do just that (Passmore 1999). However, by the time they secured power in 1997, this had been reduced to an election commitment to abolish the assisted places system, and explore ways in which independent schools and state schools might work together. Most independent schools provide excellent educational opportunities, and most parents would want these opportunities for their own children; yet not all parents can afford it.

Mike and Alex put it very succinctly in their respective quotes above. It is a classic clash of principles: equality of opportunity versus parental choice. How is it possible to sustain a belief in the right of *all* children to have the possibility of access to higher education and rewarding work if they are able enough, when it is clear that not only is access rationed, but some parents can leapfrog over others by buying their way into certain schools to enhance their children's access? Independent schools take a 50 per cent share of some university places, although only 9 per cent of children attend such schools. Is this fair?

For those who aren't concerned about fairness, perhaps there are other questions that are more appropriate. Is it effective? If parents can secure advancement for their offspring, regardless of the child's ability, is this socially efficient? 'They believed in themselves, no matter how thick they were,' comments David Blunkett about his interaction with boys from Shrewsbury public school, and goes on to acknowledge the dilemma of maintaining the principle of equality of opportunity alongside parental freedom. 'I don't disagree with either of these points,' he says in response to Jonathan and Mike's comments about fairness and choice. 'The question is, are we making any progress towards them (equalizing resources), and what are the constraints?' The Secretary of State sketches out some ways in which the public and private sector can work together, a theme on which he has elaborated in a number of policy statements as the government tries to get to grips with the problem without alienating either sector.

In an article for the *New Statesman* in July 1999, Professor Julian Le Grand from the London School of Economics considered the extent to which a committed, activist government *could* actually remove all barriers to any individual achieving his or her full potential.

We have to ensure that a family's ability to pass on excessive privilege to its children is restricted. Excellence in education has to be made available to all, not just to the sons and daughters of the better off. We cannot have the privileged buying extra advantages for their children through private schools. This does not mean abolishing private schools. There is nothing wrong with Eton as such. What is wrong is the excellence of Eton – or Westminster or Winchester – or any of the other great public schools being confined to the children of the rich. The public schools should be exactly what their name implies – public.

(Le Grand 1999)

Rather than pursuing the path of abolition, Professor Le Grand proposes that the state should go in the opposite direction and make all places at private schools 'assisted', paying for every pupil who attends such schools, on the condition that they do not accept fee-paying pupils as well. At the same time, the resources of the state sector need to be increased to match those of the private sector, so that the quality of the education in both sectors is comparable. To achieve this would require tax increases for some groups, but this might actually become politically popular, if the public schools' cherished excellence was preserved at the same time as state schools were improved. Le Grand's proposal to restrict the right to purchase private education appears to be very radical, but he draws a parallel with Canada which has already successfully legislated against private health care.

Is it really possible though to create a society where accident of birth doesn't automatically confer privileged access to wealth and success? Such a society would not deny the existence of inequalities but would recognize Charles Handy's assertion that 'capitalism only survives where people have an equal chance to access the inequalities.' If this sounds utterly and hopelessly Utopian, or even impossibly stupid, let me point to a country not so far away, where the system proposed by Julian Le Grand for the UK actually operates. Although Peter Hoeg's novels offer some interesting perspectives on the 'shadow side' of Denmark (Hoeg 1994, 1995) it is a country where all private school places *are* 'assisted' places, and where the state sector *is* extremely well resourced. Privileged access to further and higher education cannot be 'bought' through attendance at particular schools. It is open to all those who have the aptitude and commitment, whatever their background.

It has become fashionable to make comparisons between education and economic performance in the UK and countries on the other side of the globe – specifically the 'tiger economies' of Hong Kong, Singapore, Taiwan and South Korea. Closer to our shores though is a country whose economic performance is every bit as impressive as those along the Pacific Rim, and whose traditions and cultures have much in common with our own. An examination of its education system and underpinning values may be worthy of study.

With this in mind the next chapter considers the responses of Danish sixth form students to similar questions posed to the British students interviewed for Chapters 4 and 5. Their comments offer some illuminating insights.

# 14

# Danish perspectives: comments from sixth formers

Less than a thousand years ago we shared a common language and culture with the Vikings. Many of our place names and the roots of words can be traced back to this linkage – by, sted, wich, berg and haven are just some examples of suffixes attached to names of towns and villages that indicate the Viking origin. Many of us are descended directly from the Norsemen (including those that arrived from Normandy with William the Conqueror), as our own surnames indicate.

In the first chapter I made reference to the Danish system as a model from which we might take away some useful lessons. A system of 'social democracy' has predominated since the Second World War, so it is possible to evaluate the benefits and the drawbacks of more than 50 years of this Scandinavian experiment – as the Danes themselves are constantly committed to doing (Hastrup 1995). Some of the noteworthy things about Denmark include the following:

- Most Danes pay more than 50 per cent of their earnings in tax (compared to 21 per cent in the UK), yet consistently vote against political parties that offer to reduce it (Barnes 1999).
- The minimum wage is £8 an hour (compared to £3.60 in the UK), yet this hasn't created a vast pool of unemployed people.
- The average working week is 37 hours for those employed in manufacturing industry (compared to 45 in the UK), yet Denmark's competitive edge in the international market is legendary.
- Teachers are not encouraged to teach children to read until the age of 7, yet adult illiteracy levels are among the lowest in Europe.
- The first national tests that young people experience are the 'optional' examinations at 16, yet levels of attainment in mathematics and science compare favourably with young people in the UK.

- All pupils are taught in mixed ability groups from the age of 6 to 16, yet parents and teachers don't describe it as a near-impossible task that can only be achieved by particularly talented teachers.
- Parents are not allowed to hit their children, yet young people are certainly as courteous, socially responsible, and respectful of authority as children in the UK.

Denmark is a prosperous and peaceful country which, in the Estes study of quality of life in 107 nations around the world, was ranked top alongside Sweden. The UK came 37th (Estes 1984). More recently, only Canada, New Zealand and the Netherlands have vied with the Scandinavian countries as places that enjoy a higher quality of life.

As a conclusion to the interviews with young people in the UK and the adult experts, I thought it might be interesting to talk with Danish students in the final years of their schooling, to see if their experiences and observations might add anything to the debate about values and vision that is central to this book. I was curious to illuminate some of the things I've observed over a 25-year period of visiting Denmark, mostly in the context of school or university exchange programmes.

On my very first visit in 1976, as a participant at a conference on alternatives to unemployment, I was told about Christiania, a commune of around 1000 people who had taken over an abandoned army barracks and surrounding grounds close to the centre of Copenhagen. This alternative society flourished within the confines of the perimeter wall, a haven for those who wanted to drop out of the mainstream and experience a more anarchic lifestyle. Despite their rejection of Danish society and the inevitable emergence of a 'drug' culture within Christiania, the commune's right to exist was underwritten by the city authorities who voted to maintain public services such as water, electricity and sewage. Some years later my partner and I visited for ourselves. We walked through the main gates, past the line of dealers with their balls of brown–black resin, and into the unhurried calm that seemed to characterize Christiania. As we wandered past the recycling projects, the bicycle trailer construction workshop and the vegetable plots, we were struck by the friendliness of those we met. In the bakery, the smell of fresh loaves mingled with the sweetness of marijuana, the ever-present symbol of life in Christiania.

Christiania's existence seemed to epitomize a very important aspect of Danish society – in which the right to be different could be embraced by the predominant culture, without either side feeling threatened. This acceptance of difference is visible throughout the whole educational system. Although Folk Schools (equivalent to our comprehensive schools and 100 per cent funded by the state) are attended by the majority of the population, it is perfectly possible for a group of parents to set up their own school because they want more of a focus on religion or environmental issues, or sport, or democracy than they feel is present in the local Folk School. These 'free' schools will have most of their running costs paid directly by the government, although parental contributions are encouraged and expected, unless a low level of income precludes this. Poverty is not a barrier to enrolment. 15 per cent of children attend such schools.

There is no advantage to be gained in terms of access to further or higher education, but children may have an overall educational experience that is qualitatively different to that of their contemporaries attending the Folk School. Not necessarily better or worse, but different, where the ideas of Nikolai Grundtvig, a poet and clergyman and visionary of the nineteenth century, very much influence the form and content of what is on offer in many of these schools. Personal development is seen as central to the whole process. Relationships between staff and pupils and parents are highly regarded. Time is regularly set aside for social and cultural activities that involve the whole class. Feelings, creativity, spirituality, physical activity and social responsibility are encouraged and explored.

This emphasis on affective factors is very evident throughout the free school network, and to a lesser but significant extent within the whole of the rest of the educational system from kindergarten through to post-16 provision and Grundtvig is generally credited with the inspiration for this. How one person's beliefs could actually influence a whole country's educational system is a story in its own right, and one which many other writers have explored in depth (Thaning 1982 and Borish 1991 for instance). I have summarized Grundtvig's views on *oplysning* (enlightenment), *den levende ord* (the living word) and *folkelighed* (enlightenment) in *Curriculum Innovation* (White 1997).

Most of my 'professional' time in Denmark has been spent in the alternative school system, visiting, working and mixing with teachers and pupils in a variety of the 'free schools', 'after schools' and 'folk high schools' that most clearly illustrate Grundtvig's ideas through their practice. Given that the interviews with British pupils have concentrated on those with aspirations to continue in further and higher education, it seemed appropriate to identify a similar group of young people in Denmark, so I arranged to meet and interview students attending a traditional Gymnasium.

A Gymnasium is the Danish equivalent of a sixth form college. In the Danish system 93 per cent of students continue with further education and training after the age of 16. Over half of these follow a three-year course in the Gymnasium, choosing to follow either the 'mathematics line' or the 'languages line', both of which lead to a final examination in 10 subjects (most of which are common to both lines). To qualify for admission applicants must have completed nine or ten years of basic education, and achieved satisfactory results in Danish and mathematics. The previous school can be a free school, Folk School or after school, and must declare the applicant qualified for the Gymnasium. Once students reach the age of 18 they are entitled to a mandatory grant from the government of between £100 and £150 a month to assist them with their studies (Ministry of Education in Denmark 1998b).

Interestingly, although 15 per cent of Danish children attend alternative schools until the age of 16 or 17, there are no alternatives to the Gymnasium for anyone aspiring to university. It becomes the melting-pot for all young people between the ages of 16 and 20 who are keen to continue with some kind of academic education.

The students interviewed here were young men and women from across the whole three years of the Gymnasium structure. Some of their comments echo their counterparts in the UK, particularly when they are talking about the importance of friendships and the qualities they most value in effective teachers. But there are some striking differences, like their views on the age that children should learn to read, and the processes that they regard as most significant within formal schooling. When they comment on the world beyond the school walls, their views reflect the culture they have grown up in and stand as a very interesting prompt to further thought and analysis.

Their remarks speak for themselves, and the only other preface I would want to offer on what is represented below is that these were young people whose first language is Danish. In very few cases have I had to make any corrections to grammar or vocabulary. The fluency and the complexity of language and analysis is entirely theirs.

## On starting school . . .

'When I started at kindergarten at the age of 6, we just played a lot and learned a few letters and a few numbers. For the first year it was very easy: a lot of playing, sitting in circles, and a lot of fun. Then I remember starting in the first grade (age 7) and I thought, "Well OK, now it's going to get harder, there's going to be a lot of pressure." But there really wasn't. I looked forward to going to school every day.'

(Julia)

'I started in the kindergarten class two months later than the rest of my class because I wasn't ready. I remember that we learned how to tell the time and tie our shoe laces.'

(Asbjorn)

'I remember that my teacher painted faces for all her new students. What is good about school is that you learn new things every day and you have people around you that you like – your friends.'

(Rine)

'On the first day I was very afraid of having to learn German. But we didn't do that in the first class. And then I thought we had a really old teacher because she didn't look like the other people I talked to. You can see that I was a bit confused on my first day.'

(Katrine B.)

'Children in England don't have so much time to fool around as we have. I saw a programme on the telly once, which showed these small kids and their parents' expectations were so high. It mattered if a child wasn't performing well. I'm very happy that I had the possibility to play all day when I was 5. I like watching children playing around, making a noise. I think they are supposed to.'

(Mona)

'I think it's important that kids have their time to play when they are kids. They are going to be grown-ups fast enough. They need to get used to school, so they don't find it scary. The kindergarten classes are a good way of learning how everything works in a school.'

(Lilian)

'I actually started when I was 5, a year earlier than normal, because all my friends were starting then. I really looked forward to going. Then I had to do one more year in kindergarten. It was all right.'

(Helene)

'I also started when I was 5. My parents thought that I was bored because all my friends were a year older and they were at school. I really wanted to go to school. I only did one year at kindergarten though, so I was always a year younger than everyone else in my class. In that first year we played, we learnt to sing, we drew pictures. We started to learn to read and write when we were 7. Some kids come too early to school. Some of them are just wild and they are too young to sit down on a chair.'

(Ann-Karin)

'It was easy going to school in the beginning. It was very practical. We played, we sang, we talked, we made things. Reading and writing came later. If you start too young, I'd be worried that children would be too scared to start language. It gave me confidence believing I could do the things I was asked to do. What mattered most to me was being with my friends.'

(Kristian)

## On learning to read . . .

'At 7 or 8 you start learning small words like cat and hat, and then in the third grade (age 10) we started reading small books. I think it's extremely early to start teaching children to read when they are 4 or 5, as you do in England. Some children are not even really talking at that age. If they start learning to read when they are 4 years old, what do they do when they come to school? When I started kindergarten I was ready to go to school; I was ready to start learning to read and write. My parents didn't press me in any way, but I was ready and a bit further along than many others in my class. I remember the first time in my first grade when I got an assignment I had to for homework, I felt very proud and very grown up just because I had homework. It's not like that any more though!'

(Julia)

'I loved it because we had a lot of friends and it was not difficult. You were good friends with the teacher. We made things; we played a lot. A lot of people would think it's not too easy to start learning to read before the first class. Seven is a good age.'

(Merete)

'I remember telling my little sister the alphabet when she was 5, before she started school, but I don't think I knew the alphabet before I started. I don't think you should start earlier. You get tired of school soon enough, so I don't think you should protract it.'

(Anne)

'I liked it. I thought it was interesting, the teachers were cool, and we played a lot. I think it's bad for children to have to learn to read when they are very young. When you are so small you have to fool around, learn how to get on with other children through playing.'

(Lonni)

'The trouble is that researchers say that Danish pupils are very bad readers. Investigations of 10-year-olds show that Danish pupils are not as good at reading as children in England. So maybe it's a good idea to start reading at an early age. Perhaps the sooner you start the more you learn.'

(Torsten)

'I think it's important to have fun in the first year at school, to make drawings, play ball, and so on, before you start learning to read.'

(Jacob)

'I started to read and write when I was 6. I don't think it's necessary to learn to read when children are 4 years old. But it is a problem for Danish schools that in a lot of European countries children are taught to read from the age of 4. Because we don't do that in Denmark, we are a bit behind. Some say it's more relaxed in Danish schools, but I don't know if that means you learn more. Certainly it shouldn't be a problem for children if they don't read straight away.'

(Rine)

'You can't say that when children are all 6 that they're all ready. It hasn't got to do with age.'

(Karen)

## On class sizes . . .

'The class sizes are twice as big in the Gymnasium as they were in the Folk School. In the beginning we were 28 in my group, and in my Folk School we were 14 in the class.'

(Lonni)

'The first eight years there were six of us in my class. And then I started at a new school where we were 25, so that was very, very different. I liked the small size because you got to know each other very well. You dared to say things, you didn't just sit there. You have to do your homework and speak up in class, because you can't hide. Here you can hide because there are so many people in each class. Most of us are in classes of 20 or more, and I think that's too many. It helped me a lot to be in class with just six others when I was at the Folk School. I have no problems standing up in front of the class here at the Gymnasium. And I'm not afraid of asking stupid questions. I do that a lot of times.'

(Anne)

'There were 17 people in my class and I liked it because we were with the same people for eight years. We didn't change teachers until the fifth grade. Of course when there's a small number and you're together for five years, you can sometimes get pretty furious with each other. But if you had an argument, you could always talk to someone else.'

(Merete)

'We were 28 in our class, which was too many. But then along came two other pupils and because we were 30 they had to split us up. So we were 14 and 16.'

(Lilian)

'I went to school in a village about ten kilometres from here. It's what we call a free school. At first there were five or six in the class, then there were only three. Sometimes we had classes with the ones above us. It was OK, it worked. Sometimes we had lessons on our own. The things we could do together, we did together.'

(Katrine R.)

**On assessment and competition . . .**

'At the Folk School we are called in with our parents to talk with the teachers. That way you can get a picture of where you are in the class. The teacher can tell you if there are some things that you need to do better, and which things you're doing well at. You get a picture of where you are. Marks are not made public though. I think that's good, because if you get a bad grade I don't think the others have a right to know. You can decide to tell them if you want to.'

(Ole)

'You know how other people are doing because you're sitting in class when the teachers are asking people questions and you might read their homework. But if we sit down and take a maths test I wouldn't know if Kristian did well or badly, unless he chose to tell me. You will never see lists of grades put up in Denmark, not even for exams – never.'

(Julia)

'There are no lists that compare students. Each student gets his own grades and he doesn't have to show it to others.'

(Torsten)

'I guess I was somewhere in the middle at Folk School. I began to realize how good I was in terms of subjects when I was 10 or 11. We didn't get grades, but the teacher would put a mark to show that she was satisfied – so you knew whether it was good or bad work. It wasn't something you got nervous about.'

(Merete)

'If you are not that good you will know. We have some afternoons after school where people can go and get help. The teacher will come to you if he thinks you have a problem in some subject and say, "I'm there between this and this hour. I think you need to be there. Because if you don't you're not going to make it in this subject." '

(Julia)

'I took my first test when I was 13, and the first notes about my grades went home to my parents at that time. In the eighth and ninth classes some of my teachers put the best student names on the blackboard. I don't think that was a good thing, because it made them rather like heroes. It isn't helpful for the students who aren't that good to see that their names are not on the blackboard.'

(Asbjorn)

'The grades weren't put up on the board in my school. You could keep it to yourself. You knew how other people did, because we talked,

"Hey, what did you get? I got this." And then everyone knew. Even without that you could feel how good people were in the class.'

(Lilian)

'I don't think it helps to put names up on the blackboard. Some people will tease them as well and say, "Oh, you are just doing everything, you are so sweet!"'

(Katrine B.)

'The teachers want everyone to be equal. In the old days we had this system where if you were very good you had to sit at the front of the class, the stupid ones at the back. Today it's the other way round. If someone is finding things difficult, they have to be helped. This happens in all classes if someone is not as good as the others. If school was a race to get the highest grades, it would not be fun.'

(Jacob)

'I think it's too early to put children into different classes according to how good they are at school work, when they're in the Folk School. I think it should be later than at 12 or 13. At that age most boys don't really do much about their homework, while most girls sit down and do it.'

(Anne)

'It is expected that pupils will help each other in the Folk School. And it's like that here as well. If somebody has problems and another one can do it, the teachers find it great if we help each other. We are all very good at being happy for someone who does well. And sad if someone does badly. We really were sad because there was a girl in our class who got five (a fail grade) in mathematics.'

(Lonni)

'It would be nice if it was OK to just stand up and say, "Hey, I'm doing fine; I'm earning money, I'm having success," but it's not always OK to do that in Denmark. You are supposed to keep a low profile. You have to be like everybody else; you have to act like other people. In school it means you don't go round saying, "I got eleven," because you know there might be one student over there who only got five or something like that. I think it's wrong if you have to feel guilty because you did something well. But sometimes you do feel guilty. When you get excited about getting good marks, you don't think about it when you're actually in the situation, but afterwards you think, "Oh, I shouldn't have done that".'

(Anne)

'There's not competition between the students here, but we have to think about our grades if we want to do particular jobs. If I want to study to be a doctor, I need to get certain grades. But we help each other, and that's great. Sometimes we do essays together.'

(Mona)

'I don't think we feel so much in competition with each other. We don't have the need to be "the best". There's a boy in our class who speaks with a lot of difficult words. We just say, "Oh, he has been reading the dictionary." We don't think he is better than us just because he can use those words.'

(Katrine R.)

'We have two girls in my class. They are pretty smart, both of them. They are sometimes fighting to be better than each other; you can hear it in the class. Most of us think that it is silly. We don't agree and we don't like it. There's nothing wrong with trying to do their best, but they are getting too mean with each other.'

(Karen)

'I think it's healthy to have grades here. Because if we didn't have grades, students would not do their homework. But it shouldn't happen in the early years of the Folk School. For us it started in the fifth grade.'

(Katrine R.)

'It was a shock for me to come to the Gymnasium because suddenly I had to compete with all these people for the first time. I was not used to that at all. If you're not used to it, you kind of push it back, you don't need it, you don't want it.'

(Ann Karin)

'Being at school is a lot about learning how to be with people, and coping with competition and stuff like that.'

(Julia)

**On teachers . . .**

'Good teachers need to have a sense of humour, but at the same time they need to be strict. They need to respect you, love teaching, like children.

(Katrine R.)

'It's important that the teacher can talk to a student, not just in the class, but also during the breaks. If you have something you're worried about and you can talk to a teacher about it, that's very important. If you can't do that, you might get behind.'

(Ann Karin)

'Teachers need to be relaxed, kind and interesting.'

(Katrine B.)

'They have to be able to stop noise.'

(Rine)

'Teachers who just burn for their subject are the best. There are some who are boring and kind of "I am here today, I get my pay, and you are sitting there trying to learn . . . I do not care." Those are the worst.'

(Ole)

'What matters is that they have a passion for their subject and a way of motivating you. Some teachers have the ability to motivate people, to know just how far they can push it, how provoking they can be to make you this close to giving up, but you then decide, "I'm going to show this teacher." I had an amazing teacher who I didn't particularly like, but I respected him for the way he teaches. He made every single student in his class live up to their absolute best.'

(Julia)

'What matters is that teachers keep us motivated and give us the inspiration to work, so that you don't get bored in class.'

(Kristian)

'A good teacher is one who is interested in learning. What matters is the ability to engage your interest. If the teacher sometimes comes up with a joke, then we have a laugh, and we want to learn more. Teachers need to be able to listen and try to see things from other points of view than just their own. You need to have your own opinions valued.'

(Mona)

'Our class teacher was very good. She wasn't strict and you could talk to her about everything. She was somewhere between a mother and friend to us. If somebody didn't understand what she was teaching, she helped everyone so that we were equal. She would always help the ones who had difficulty following the lesson.'

(Merete)

'The teachers I like are the ones who are kind to us. But some teachers only care about their subject and haven't got a human sense at all. It's a bit hard to learn from teachers like that.'

(Katrine B.)

'Teachers should feel it's a pleasure to teach us, that it's something they enjoy. If the children don't understand, the teacher says, "OK, well if you try to look at it like this . . ." Of course you have to know your subject. Some teachers don't have the knowledge or the interest. It's incredible how teachers can affect whether you like a subject or not.'

(Helene)

'I didn't like maths until I had a particular teacher ... and I really respected him and I liked him. And I learned a lot. But suddenly it changed and I got another teacher and I just hated maths again.'

(Anon)

## Differences between the Folk School and the Gymnasium ...

'It's more personal between teachers and students in the Folk School. We have our class teacher for many years and maybe a Danish teacher for Danish lessons. That way we get a very good relationship with our class teacher. She will maybe ask, "How is your mother today?" Something like that.'

(Karen)

'It's more professional and not so emotional in the Gymnasium. But I like it when teachers come in and say, "Hey, come on, let's hear what you think about this. And did you have a nice trip this weekend?" and so on.'

(Mona)

'Compared with the Folk School the teachers in the Gymnasium are less involved with us. In the Folk School we had the same teachers for five or six years, so we had a personal relationship, which was very relaxed.'

(Ole)

'The Folk School is something that everyone has to go to. The Gymnasium is something you select, so it is expected you work more seriously.'

(Torsten)

'It's more grown up in the Gymnasium.'

(Jacob)

'We have to make ourselves do the work here. In the Folk School the teachers would really get cross if we didn't do our homework, our essays and so on, but now it's our own problem.'

(Mona)

'The teachers are not so involved with their students as in the Folk School. It seems as if teachers like you in the Folk School. Here they come in, they teach you something, and then they walk out again. Actually that's OK, because you are more interested in the subject than in the teacher at the Gymnasium. But you can't go to the teacher and say, "My God, I feel like shit today, that's why I'm not saying anything." It just doesn't work that way.'

(Lonni)

'The relationship between the students and the teachers is very different here. It's very distant. The teachers often seem to think that we didn't learn anything in the Folk School. I think that's very irritating to hear, because of course you must have learnt something. You can't have gone to school for nine years and not learnt anything! It would be good if we could have more open discussions like we had in the Folk School. Here the teacher's opinion is always the right one, especially when you're analysing a text or something like that. If you come up with your own opinions, you don't really get the chance to say why you think so.'

(Anne)

'It seems like there's a wall between teachers and the students. They just talk to each other in the classes about the subject and not anything else. But there's something good about that in a way, because there has to be a distance between teachers and students. Sometimes it seems too big; sometimes you forget that teachers are humans too.'

(Merete)

'In the Gymnasium they teach to a group. In the Folk School they teach each student. In the Folk School I had some difficulty with one of my subjects. The teacher read the text into a tape and I took it home, put it in the tape recorder and sat there listening to it, reading out loud. That helped me wonderfully. But I don't think teachers in the Gymnasium would do the same thing. OK, you might say, if you need as much help as that, you shouldn't be in the Gymnasium!'

(Asbjorn)

'In the Folk School they are more concerned about how you feel. Now we are grown ups, so we have to take care of ourselves. When we were only kids the teachers have to be like a mum and dad. But that's not how it is here.'

(Lilian)

'It's more serious at Gymnasium. In the Folk School you have to de-velop your personality. It's not so much about learning things. They are not so strict.'

(Jacob)

'We have the opportunity to choose to do the tenth grade in Folk School, and I did that because I was a year younger than everybody else. You could also go straight into the Gymnasium from the ninth grade. But I stayed on because I thought my personality was not so developed. I didn't really think it was anything to do with my brains; it was about how mature I was. Something different happens in your life when you start going to the Gymnasium. It's not the same. Mind you I've regretted it now, because I would have liked to have finished this summer, but

I've got one more year. If everyone had to start school when they were 5 like me, then I wouldn't have had to do this extra year!'

(Helene)

'One big difference is that the state pays people to go to the Gymnasium when they are over 18. You get a certain amount of money each month, depending on whether or not you live with your parents.'

(Kristian)

## Plans for what to do after finishing at the Gymnasium . . .

'There are two jobs I'd like to do. One is interior designer, and the other is archaeologist. I've always been fascinated by the thought of discovering something new from the past.'

(Ole)

'I would like to study physics or chemistry at university, and then there are many different job possibilities – in teaching or in industry.'

(Torsten)

'I want to be a lawyer. I think there are some people who get off too easily!'

(Lonni)

'I would like to be an optician, but I plan to go travelling first.'

(Merete)

'I am thinking about being an engineer, but I want to travel first as well.'

(Anne)

'I would like to work in a hotel for one year and travel abroad before going to university to study to be a doctor.'

(Rine)

'I want to earn some money first. Then I don't know whether I will go travelling or go to a Folk High School where you can live and be together with other people. After that I think I will go to university to become a pharmacist.'

(Lilian)

'When I'm finished here I would like to travel. Work for a while and go to Australia. Then I'd like to be an architect.'

(Katrine B.)

'I would like to go to university, but maybe I'll take a year at business school first. I'd like to be an architect too.'

(Asbjorn)

## On issues beyond school ...

'One of the biggest political issues at this time concerns refugees, immigrants. I think we ought to help them a lot more than we do today. We should teach them to speak Danish, the Danish way of life and so on. I also think the law should be changed so that it is easier to get permission to be a Danish citizen. You say we are world famous for being tolerant as a country. Today we see that's only a rumour. Danes are not so tolerant after all. The third biggest political party in Denmark is a party that says all the immigrants and refugees should be thrown out of the country right now. It's a racist party. I think people are afraid that Denmark will become multi-ethnic, but in 1849 when we made the first democratic laws, we said you are allowed to believe in what you want. It's an important principle. Anyway we are such a small generation – those of us born in '81, '82, '83. In a few years a third of the population will be over 60 and the state will need to pay for them. But the working population is going down. I think immigrants and refugees are just what we need. We need some young people who have a reason to work, because they want to start a new life.'

(Torsten)

'One of the rumours about immigrants is that they just sit around, but in fact a lot of them are working and trying to earn money. Of course there will be some who cannot get jobs themselves and we need to support them. In some countries people can actually die on the streets, while a rich man is sitting in his house. It's important to have a good social welfare system. In Denmark we pay half our income to the state, but we have good hospitals and schools. Everything is free for us.'

(Jacob)

'There are problems for older people. Not all of them can have their houses cleaned. And there are long waiting times for them to get into hospitals to get a new hip or whatever.'

(Merete)

'There's too much crime in the eastern part of Denmark, round Copenhagen. Not here. We can just leave our money on the table and go for our lessons and come back and it will still be there. At my cousin's Gymnasium, south of Copenhagen, they can't even leave a book on the table!'

(Asbjorn)

'I would like to do something about the hospitals ... and the home care for the elderly. Also our relationships to foreigners in this country. We're maybe a bit racist because we won't let them in on our jobs.'

(Karen)

'I don't think we should have private hospitals. Many people can't afford them. We pay high taxes for the public sector.'

(Kristian)

'I think it's good that we have high taxes. Otherwise we would not have all the things that we have access to.'

(Helene)

'We pay a lot of tax, so I don't think we should make it any higher. But it's good that we pay what we do because there are a lot of people who really need help and who can't afford it themselves. Like my father for instance. He has a bad back, so he needed to take a new education. He couldn't have afforded it by himself, but he was helped by the social system. That's good. I don't know what would have happened if he hadn't been able to do that. Paying taxes is important so that you know you will be OK if something goes wrong. It's important to have a hospital nearby for instance. There's talk about shutting the one here to save money, but I think that's bad because you need to have your family close by if you're old and in hospital.'

(Anne)

The above reflects some fascinating cultural differences between Denmark and the UK, and generates a number of questions, such as how it is possible to sustain a collectivist ethos in a competitive world, or how they manage the balance between academic achievement and personal growth which is clearly right at the heart of Danish education. To pursue these and other issues I arranged to interview the Minister of Education in Denmark, Margrethe Vestager. Her responses are given in the following chapter.

# Interview with Margrethe Vestager
## Minister of Education, Denmark

**Roger Crombie White**  I'd like to start by asking about your own schooling.
**Margrethe Vestager**  I went to ordinary Danish Folk Schools (what you would call combined primary and secondary schools), first in the countryside and then in a small town. I finished my basic education in what we call an *Efterskole* – a boarding school for 16- and 17-year-olds.
**R.C.W.**  Was yours a typical Danish experience, starting at age 6 and then staying with the same class teacher for most lessons until you were 14?
**M.V.**  Yes, except that I changed school when I was 11 years old, so I actually had a couple of teachers. In that respect my experience is like that of many children today, because people move more. The number of children having the same teacher from Grade 1 to Grade 9 is shrinking.
**R.C.W.**  The pattern of going to an Efterskole after 10 years at the Folkeskole, which you did, is also quite common, isn't it?
**M.V.**  It is becoming even more common. A large proportion of boarding schools have experienced a huge increase in the number of pupils over the last 10 years.
**R.C.W.**  For good reasons? Not just because parents want their 16-year-old children away from home for a year? . . .
**M.V.**  I guess there are a number of reasons and that is certainly one of them – that parents think teenagers in the middle of their puberty could gain from living away from home for a period of time. I believe they are right.
**R.C.W.**  Many parents of adolescents in Britain would think this is wonderful, but we don't have such a facility! From the Efterskole you went to the Gymnasium?
**M.V.**  Yes I did and from there I went directly to university. Like many young people I wanted to go travelling, but to travel with my education.

So I waited until I had passed what we now call the Bachelor degree before I went anywhere. It was shorter than I had originally envisaged because I got caught up in studying and working and other things. I was a trainee in the European Parliament for a period of four months. I was never really turned on by the idea of travelling round the world, spending two months in Nepal or Australia, or wherever, like a lot of young people today.

**R.C.W.** I meet very few Danish young people for whom that is not the ambition. When they leave the Gymnasium they are all going to travel. The population of Denmark must be significantly reduced because there are so many 18 to 20-year-olds not here!

**M.V.** Danes love to travel. Since the cost of airline tickets has fallen so dramatically over the last 10 years, it makes it possible. You can work six months in a bar or a factory or wherever, and you are then able to finance another six months of travelling.

**R.C.W.** Was your own overall experience of school a good one? Did you enjoy it?

**M.V.** Yes I did, although one of the basic mismatches between me and the school system was that I was the kind of child who was very interested in books and theory and reading and writing. The success criteria of the schoolyard were to do with ball-playing and running and those kind of things. Also, sometimes within the classroom it was felt that you shouldn't be too occupied with books or studying and such like.

**R.C.W.** Was this 'Jante law' at work?

**M.V.** There are a number of explanations, but the Jante law plays a part. Also, because I was the child of two church ministers I was very visible. There were a lot of expectations on one hand – and some prejudices on the other hand. Everyone knows that the child of the minister is always the worst one – at least, that's what we say in Denmark!

**R.C.W.** Although your two daughters are not yet old enough for school, what kind of schooling do you hope to arrange for them, given your own experience? Will it be the same?

**M.V.** In some respects yes, in some respects no. I will try to find one of the most progressive Danish Folk Schools – because our schools are very different. Even though we have a national system, there are a number of differences in the way that things are organized – how we use IT for example, and how much emphasis is put upon music and playing and gymnastics. I'd prefer schools which were equally focused on the knowledge which is given by books, and the knowledge and insight given by music, practical work, gymnastics and such like.

**R.C.W.** Had I asked that question of any of the Education Ministers that we have had in Britain over the past 20 years, with the exception of David Blunkett, the answer would have been to get them into one of the most reputable private schools, in order to improve their chances of access to university, and the particularly prestigious universities of Oxford and Cambridge. The answer would not have been about music, art and the kind of things that you were talking about. Is this an issue in Denmark – about buying or securing privilege through education?

**M.V.**   Very little I think.

**R.C.W.**   Why not?

**M.V.**   Because we have a very open system and all education is paid for by the public. You don't pay to go to university. We don't have very prestigious universities, but we don't have very bad universities either. They offer an equivalent level of quality. To get there, you don't have to take private school exams, you don't have to do things which cost your family extra money. I think that basically Danes believe that it should be possible to follow whichever educational route you want to take, assuming that you are prepared to do the work needed to get there.

**R.C.W.**   Are there any schools that are considered high-status Folk Schools, into which only certain sorts of people would be able to get their children?

**M.V.**   No.

**R.C.W.**   Or perhaps geographic areas where the housing is so expensive that only wealthy people live in the catchment area?

**M.V.**   Well yes, but those schools do not make claims that 'all of those who come to this school are going to have a very brilliant academic career'. The children *might* go this way because they come from an academic background, and of course we have the pattern that those who have grown up with books and an academic way of thinking are more inclined to go the same way as their parents compared to those children who have grown up in an almost literary vacuum. Even so we begin to see pattern breakers – children who are able to take other educational choices than their parents took. In that respect I also think that our two systems are very different.

**R.C.W.**   There are other differences too. The students from the Gymnasium talked a lot about the early years of schooling. When I pointed out that, in the UK, we start teaching children to read at 4 or 5, some of them were quite astounded and one or two were appalled. There were quotes like, 'If they start learning to read when they are 4 years old, what do they do when they come to school?' and, 'It's important that children have time to play when they are kids.' You must be aware of this difference between the UK and Denmark.

**M.V.**   In Denmark we try to meet the child where it is. Some 4-year-olds are very interested in learning to read and write; other children are not interested at all and are somewhere quite different. We recognize that pre-school activities and what the parents are doing with their children are both very important in relation to how the children respond at school when they start there. In organizing the teaching in the first grade we take account of this and the fact that some of them can read already, while some of them have hardly seen a letter before. We try to accommodate both kinds of children. At home my daughter Maria, who has just turned 4, is very interested in learning how to spell and what the letters are like. If I read a book aloud to her, she wants my finger to follow the lines: 'Where are you when you say these things?' Of course we accommodate her if she is interested, but we are not pushy. We don't have a programme that says when I come home we must do half an hour of reading together after dinner. Not at all.

**R.C.W.** So how does it work in schools? Most children start at the age of 6. Some can read, others can't. It seems rather like a train standing at a station. You wait until everyone is ready before moving off through the academic programme. Is that how it is?

**M.V.** In some respects that is a correct picture. We are trying to get better at differentiating the way of teaching. In the eighties teachers might have had a way of pedagogical thinking which was a little laid back: 'It will come, sooner or later they will learn to read and write; give them peace, let them be children, they have to play and so on.' But then some international research at the beginning of the nineties showed that the level of Danish children was very bad, so we had an intense and critical debate about the skill of actually reading and writing. We saw a pedagogical change. 'If you think about what you want to do and you do it in a good way, then you can both let the children play and be children and you can also teach them to read and write. You can make it possible for those who are very motivated from the beginning to move forward, but you can also make it possible for the rest to catch up.'

**R.C.W.** That's quite difficult?

**M.V.** Yes, because it challenged the methodology of the teachers. It was introduced in the law of 1993, and slowly but surely has become reality.

**R.C.W.** What was driving this pedagogical change that you talk about? Was it fear about literacy levels? From the outside, it seems like you have a very good system.

**M.V.** I think that some Danes were very insecure about whether or not the Folk School equipped children with the basics. In an international context and in a globalized world, with competition from abroad, they weren't certain that the Danish school system was actually giving the children the competences that they needed.

**R.C.W.** Yet international tests of children of 14 or 15 don't show that Danish children are lacking in mathematics or science?

**M.V.** No, not in mathematics and science but in Danish, in the third grade, the results seemed to suggest that we did not have the world champion school system that we thought we had.

**R.C.W.** That's at 10 though, after only three years of formal schooling, compared to five or even six years in the UK, and four or five years in most other countries?

**M.V.** Nevertheless the Danish self-perception was that we had the world champion of school systems and somehow this research challenged that belief. It was a very polarized debate, with some people saying that they have to read and write and do maths, and the other side saying they have to cooperate, develop themselves, and figure out their place in the world. It has levelled out and we have settled on a balance between personal development and actual skills. Interestingly, things are changing. What you would call soft competences before, such as being able to participate in democracy, are becoming the hard competences necessary for getting a foothold in the labour market. So we are trying to make a balance between the two and see them as an integrated part of the whole educational system. The aim is to give children basic skills and abilities through reading, writing, mathematics, geography and physics and, at the same time, give them the space to develop as human beings.

**R.C.W.** To maintain a balance between personal development and actual skills has implications for the kind of teachers you need. One thing in common between the students here and students in Britain is the stress they all place on the importance of the 'passion' of a good teacher. 'Teachers who just burn for their subject are the best,' says Ole. Yet in the UK, in recent years, partly as a result of media focus on negative remarks by government ministers and employees, the status of teaching has fallen. At the moment we are struggling to recruit teachers. Is it the same in Denmark?

**M.V.** Partly. In some respects teachers have tried to hop on the wagon of industrialist thinking, so that they see teaching as being a sort of worker in a factory. 'I get my pay, I get my scheme, I have to work these and these hours.' But you cannot look on being a teacher simply as a job. It might not be a calling, but something in between. Your role is challenged, because the natural authority which came from society in earlier times is not there any more. You have to be there with your own authenticity, your own personality, your own professionalism, and establish your own authority on a day-to-day basis. The status is slowly, but gradually, increasing. We are planning a reform of the educational level of teachers, to make sure that they are more involved in research on educational process, teaching process, ICT in schools, and such like, so that more of this is infused into the system.

**R.C.W.** You mention 'being able to take part in democracy' as a core competence. That has always seemed to me, as an observer, something that is quite strong in the Danish system, right from the early years. You encourage children to do this very successfully. But I suspect *that* sort of international comparison has never been made. It's usually the formal basic skills that are tested, not the ability to be a good citizen. Is there a danger that this refocusing on basic skills is going to affect their ability to participate in a democracy?

**M.V.** The danger is certainly there, but we are trying to maintain a balance so as to keep focusing on democratic competences. I have just put a proposal to the *Folketing* (Danish parliament) to make sure that the democratic competences and possibilities for students to develop them all the way through the educational system are there in three respects. First, that all education should have education in democracy as part of the goal. Second, that the way that you teach should be democratic in its basic thinking and processes. Third, that students have access to and membership of advisory bodies to Ministers and to the *Folketing*, to make sure that they are represented all the way through the democratic system.

**R.C.W.** One of the very good international comparisons is that participation of Danish young people in 'pressure group' organizations of various sorts is very high.

**M.V.** It's higher than in most countries, but of course, as a politician, you are never really satisfied at a national level and we would like to strengthen the democratic participation even more.

**R.C.W.** Another interesting thing that the Gymnasium students kept saying – which relates to this issue of democracy and core skills – was how it took quite a long time before they realized that they were being assessed. 'There are no lists that compare students. Each student gets his own grades and he doesn't have to show it to others'; 'If school was a race to get the highest grades, it would not be fun.' They talked a lot about how they were vaguely aware that they were doing well or badly, but nobody publicized this in a competitive way. As you know, in the UK we are very strong on publishing lists and making comparisons between pupils and between schools.

**M.V.** Yes. We don't do that. We think of it as absolutely bad. We would rather use any evaluation of the quality of schools as a tool for more creative development of that quality. I think that being number 1664 in a list of schools is not very motivating. However, being told where you are, being given tools to help you take steps forward, and being given an organizational and democratic structure so that you can yourself be the initiators of a process that makes things better will develop the school system more effectively.

**R.C.W.** So it's more of a private discussion between the parties involved?

**M.V.** Yes, there are two levels of discussion. The first is between schools and local authorities. Each school should of course know where they are. We need to do evaluations and we need to do it openly. But we don't need to make a ranking between schools, because such a ranking might undermine the motivation of teachers, school leaders and municipalities to take a leadership role in further developing the school. Secondly, at the pupil level, you can have a written assessment, but more typically you have a discussion between teacher, parent and pupil, about how you are doing, what are you really good at, what you could do better, and how would you do this. We don't have any formal, national testing until the eighth, ninth or tenth grade.

**R.C.W.** In certain respects there seems to be a huge philosophical difference between our two countries. Have you heard of the phrase 'naming and shaming' which is now part of the popular language in Britain? Failing schools are publicly humiliated.

**M.V.** I don't think the humiliation part does any good.

**R.C.W.** What is particularly interesting is that, as you know, we now don't have a Conservative administration. Yet their belief system about this has been inherited by a government that is broadly equivalent to your Social Democrats.

**M.V.** The history of the two countries is very, very different. Because England has been an empire, some of that imperial thinking is part of your culture. Denmark has for many years been influenced by an egalitarian way of thinking and a very strong focus on the individual within the community. The individual should be given possibilities but within a defined framework. It is not about competition between individuals in a liberal economy.

**R.C.W.** However, if you look at the headline aims of Danish education, and the aims of British education, they are not dissimilar. The statements are about broad, balanced experiences for students, preparation for adult and working life, and so on. The written aims could be interchangeable, but the reality in the schools is quite different. You say, 'It's historic and related to empire.' Yet nine hundred years ago we were the same nation. Both countries developed imperialistic ambitions, because Denmark had a huge navy as well and an agricultural economy – very much like Britain. But something happened in the eighteenth or nineteenth centuries.

**M.V.** Denmark shrank much quicker than England. Therefore Danes had to have a very bottom-up approach to developing the way of being Danish and the economic basis of the country. I think you have a very much stronger drive towards centralism in England than you have here.

**R.C.W.** When I read *The Land of the Living* by Steven Borish it seemed to me to offer a very good account of the transformation from absolute monarchy to democracy and how that happened without bloodshed.

**M.V.** There's a lot of dimensions at play here. One of the things that Grundtvig pointed out was that such a thing as climate plays together with history, and both play together with the norms and the values of society to give the solutions that you choose. The Danes have never really been that much into revolutions! Some of the Danish values – what we really cherish – come from the way our climate is. We appreciate being together in the home, with the candles alight in the middle of the table (as I have here): the cosiness, the friendliness, the interdependence on one another. Because the country quickly became very small and everybody was related to one another, there is a familiarity between Danes.

**R.C.W.** Does Reddy's description of Danes as functioning like a large tribe explain some of your attitudes? (Reddy 1993) When I asked the Gymnasium students about taxation, they demonstrated a very sophisticated understanding of the relationship between high taxation and social benefits. There is no reluctance to continue to pay for it. That's quite remarkable. I can see that it might be one of the problems for Denmark in relation to the rest of the EU. I can understand the Danish reluctance about being a member, because it could mean a *lowering* of some very high standards.

**M.V.** Yes, it could. The reason that the Social Democratic Party grew so big, and has been the governing power for so long, is that the idea of solidarity with one another and the idea that a society needs coherence to be a society, was rooted many, many years ago. Therefore there is very little reluctance to pay taxes because you know you are part of a community. We have found some good solutions and we want to keep them.

**R.C.W.** Yes, there is certainly a strong sense of that solidarity. What do you see as the most pressing priorities for you as Minister of Education? What is it you want to change and move forward in relation to Danish education?

**M.V.** There are huge challenges at all levels of the educational system. Firstly, I want to make sure that the Folk School keeps developing an understanding of a multi-dimensional way of thinking, to make sure that it is a school for all children and that all children can find a place for developing their strong sides and from there get a jumping-off point to take hold of their less strong sides. Secondly, to make sure that the Danish school, as the prime bearer of our cultural attitudes and values, continues to be broadly accepted as the basic schooling. Thirdly, to enhance the quality and coherence within the educational system, so as to make sure that you go through a system that supports *you* and you're not just part of the machinery.

We need to make sure that we try to set aside the pictures we have inherited from the industrial society, like about mass education, to make sure that it is education for the individual in a collective framework. Grown-ups need to be given still better opportunities to come back to a learning situation, both within education and training institutions and also in connection with their labour market experience and their day-to-day work. How can the labour market and the educational system support the individual in keeping on learning and gaining new competences? I think this is very important, because even though the Danish basic school system gets better, we can't leave the grown-ups as a closed group and say, 'We give up, you have to sail your own way.' We must also make sure that those who are functionally illiterate are given proper courses which meet their needs and recognize the fact that they *are* grownups – that they have two children, an old car and the same kind of debts as their teacher. We must try to develop ways and methods of accommodating the needs of the individual and the needs of society under the same arch (Vestager 2000).

**R.C.W.**    Thank you very much.

# Conclusion

'My sisters and I went into the future and we saw fewer cars because fuel had been banned. We also saw no wars because they thought it was not nice. Also it was a lot hotter, so there were strawberries all year round. All the buildings were multi-coloured, including the houses. Later we went home and told Mum, but she didn't believe us.'

Geraldine Sherwin, age 7, in *Our World 2000*
(Save the Children 1999)

'I think kids will rule the universe. Instead of adults teaching children, children will teach adults how to be a kid, e.g. not tidying your room, not eating your dinner and only eating sweets and chocolate . . . I know you don't believe me but when kids take over the world, anything can happen.'

Roisin O'Reilly, age 10, in *Our World 2000*
(Save the Children 1999)

A recurring theme in this book has been the interplay between values and vision and the implications for what follows. '*Il faut agir.*' Action is needed on a number of levels.

At a curriculum level, we need to look at the balance between knowledge and competence, at whether the emphasis on knowing 'that' needs to give more ground in acknowledging the importance of knowing 'how'. Alongside this we need to be courageous in our responses to the insights offered by those studying the process of learning. The concept of multiple intelligence is just one aspect of this; there are many others, such as the significance of the environment, the influence of the subconscious, the power of belief (or lack of it) and the role of the teacher in lubricating the process of learning. Bruner, Vygotsky, Dewey and many others have illuminated some aspects of this, but the science of learning is still in its infancy.

We need to look at the way learning is organized and what we can do to help those who clearly need additional support, through learning mentors, gifted and talented fast-track programmes, innovative use of ICT and such like. We need to enable our many excellent teachers to have more time for teaching by releasing them from much of the routine administration that drains energies. The 'professional' role needs enhancing and the pay needs to reflect the high level of responsibility carried by teachers and schools. We need to apply a fair funding formula that acknowledges the very real difficulties some schools are experiencing in handling a disadvantaged intake. Poverty should no longer be such a determinant of performance. We need to make it much more possible for adults to come back into education and training at any point in their lives, so that it ceases to be a front-loaded system. Lifelong learning needs to become part of everyone's expectations and vocabulary (Barber 1997). In many respects the government has begun to tackle all of these. Excellence in Cities, Sure Start, New Deal, University for Industry, and Education Action Zones are a beginning; but the same approach needs to be applied to all schools and colleges throughout the UK in response to need.

Class sizes need tackling, not through a blanket formula that can actually penalize good practice as has happened in some areas with the government commitment to reduce all classes of 4- to 7-year-olds to less than 30. In many primary schools small reception classes were already in place through a judicious reallocation of resources from the later years to the early years. Such innovation deserved to be rewarded, but in some cases their foresight actually lost them funding. In Denmark the maximum class size for those in the 6–16 age group is 28 and most are around 20. Larger teaching groups come at the post-16 level, by which time young people are arguably more self-motivated.

We need to look at the methods of assessment we use. In an interview for *Tales out of School*, I recall David Hargreaves saying that 'secondary education won't move in the right direction until we've abolished all public exams before A level' (White with Brockington 1983) a sentiment he reaffirmed in his first interview shortly after the announcement of his appointment as chief executive of QCA (Cassidy 2000b). Twenty years ago that seemed rather radical. In the twenty-first century other voices have joined the chorus, including the general secretary of the Secondary Heads Association who sees the GCSE examination system at 16 as 'increasingly irrelevant' (Dunford 2000), and the Qualifications and Curriculum Authority who want to allow more 14-year-olds to choose job-related courses as an alternative to GCSEs (Cassidy 2000a). Young people in England and Wales spend more time on exams than students in any other European country (LSE 1999; Rafferty 1999), yet international comparisons of overall performance show British students to be pretty mediocre.

We need the courage to ask if all this assessment is really worth it. It is certainly good business for the examination boards who have a vested interest in resisting the demise of GCSE. But there would be huge savings in teacher time and student angst if GCSEs became an optional exam, not to mention the £50,000 saved from the examinations budget for each school each year. Why do schools and colleges pay awarding bodies to tell them they've failed with a percentage of their children? (Higham 1998) In some cases this is a very large percentage. Is it necessary? Is it wise? Since the majority of 14-year-olds continue through to 18 or 19 with some form of education or training, there is really no need to maintain a system which only had meaning when 16 was the educational endpoint for 75 per cent of young people.

We could see an end to the age-relatedness of qualifications and the demise of the performance tables that have been so destructive to professional energies of teachers. We could envisage a much broader and more exciting post-16 programme which bridges the academic and vocational divide (Pring 1995; Blunkett 2000; Tate 2000). In Birmingham, primary school children are encouraged to sit GCSE mathematics if they're ready; the dyke of fixed-age examinations in schools has been breached. Further and higher education should be seen as right for all those who can achieve the basic requirements, and the funding support needs to be there. As the Danish students have explained, their educational system thrives without any formal assessment of children before they are 16, access to further and higher education is not rationed, and all 18-year-olds qualify for a grant. There *are* creative alternatives to the current arrangements.

Permeating all the above is a need to grasp the issue of inequality. There are huge differentials in resourcing between independent schools and the state sector and between schools within the state sector. With a government committed to social justice, and wedded to the notion of 'targets' (Cohen 2000), it is quite possible to agree and define a minimum standard of resources, staffing, state of buildings, equipment and funding by which all schools can be measured as adequate (or inadequate). Those that are inadequate need to be brought up to a level of resourcing that meets the base requirements, and central government needs to foot the bill from its revenue budget (Dean 1999). Danish schools did this years ago. If access to higher education is available to all those who meet the benchmark, and funds are available to support those universities who consciously broaden their social class intake, there will be less incentive to expand the private school network and more and more of these excellent schools can become supported through public funds, to the point where all places are 'assisted places'. We could reach a situation where privileged advancement on the grounds of wealth is a thing of the past (Le Grand 1999).

In order to do this we need to grasp the nettle of taxation. In Denis Healey's famous phrase, we need to 'legislate against greed'. As a nation we have been childish in our approach to taxation (although the tide may have finally turned). We have steadfastly voted for politicians who have promised to 'cut the burden of taxation' to the point where (with the exception of the Liberal Democrats) the major political parties have been terrified of the 'tax and spend' label, and we have watched our public services crumble. Realization has slowly dawned that there is a connection between levels of taxation and provision of social welfare from which everyone benefits, and that some form of redistributive system is socially just. More importantly perhaps, there is a growing awareness that we are all winners if we can create a more cohesive society. The Danes have known this for years (McCarthy 1999) and more and more commentators (across all shades of the press) are beginning to voice a concern that higher taxation must be introduced (Wilby 1998, 2000; Sieghart 2000). There are signs that the majority of voters would support the notion of 'hypothecated' taxation.

Education has a major role to play here in establishing the 'first and public language of citizenship' that David Hargreaves refers to. We all need to become winners. Somehow we need to create a sense that we are all part of the same society – that there *is* an interconnectedness – that the quality of empathy needs to be highly valued again: it could be any one of us wrapped in a blanket on the street corner or in some other parlous state. Accident of birth and fortuitous choice points combine to endow privilege, and we need to acknowledge the responsibility that comes with such privilege both within the UK and at a global level (Barber 2000).

I am conscious that some of this sounds almost pious but I am not advocating a 'sackcloth and ashes' response to the challenges we face. As David Blunkett says, we can all be winners if we can recognize our 'common humanity'. It brings me back full circle to the issues raised in Chapter 1. We have a unique opportunity: a government committed to social justice, a strong economy, a nation that would dearly love to be at ease with itself, a population that demonstrably cares in all sorts of ways. If the values underpinning all this can combine to create a vision for schooling that excites us all, we can bequeath to our children and grandchildren the 'better world' that was in our hearts and minds at the stroke of midnight on 1 January 2000.

# Bibliography

ASDAN (Award Scheme Development and Accreditation Network) (2000) ASDAN successfully enhances GCSE provision and counters exclusion, *Newsletter*, Spring 2000. ASDAN, 27 Redland Hill, Bristol BS6 6UX.

Ayer, A. (1936) *Language, Truth and Logic*. London: Victor Gollancz.

Barber, M. (1994) *Young People and their Attitudes to School*. Interim report of a research project in the Centre for Successful Schools. Keele: Keele University.

Barber, M. (1996) Steady funding growth is key to success, *Times Educational Supplement*, 10 May.

Barber, M. (1997) *The Learning Game*. London: Cassell Group.

Barber, M. (2000) Everyone has a mountain to climb, *Times Educational Supplement*, 21 January: 21.

Barnard, N. (2000) Grammars' success discounted, *Times Educational Supplement*, 5 November: 9.

Barnes, H. (1999) Muted debate where the consensus rules, *Financial Times*, 17 December: 12.

Bayliss, V. (1998) *Redefining Schooling: A challenge to a Closed Society*. London: Royal Society of Arts.

Bayliss, V. (1999) *Opening Minds: Education for the 21st Century*. London: Royal Society of Arts.

Bentley, T. and Seltzer, K. (1999a) *The Creative Age*. London: Demos.

Bentley, T. and Seltzer, K. (1999b) Make room for creativity, *Times Educational Supplement*, 8 October: 19.

Blishen, E. (1969) *The School that I'd Like*. London: Penguin Education.

Blunkett, D. (2000) *Raising Aspirations in the 21st Century*. London: DfEE publications.

Blunkett, D. with MacCormick, A. (1995) *On A Clear Day*. London: Michael O'Mara Books.

Borish, S. (1991) *The Land of the Living*. London: Blue Dolphin Publishing.

Bragg, M. (1999) The lending of wisdom, *Times Educational Supplement*, 16 July: 15.

Brighouse, T. (1994) The magicians of the inner city, *Times Educational Supplement*, 22 April: 29–30.

Brighouse, T. (1999) Success for schools not failure – what will they look like in 2020? The Moray House Lecture, Edinburgh University, 1 October.

Bright, M. (1999) Cheating parents face fines for fraud, *Observer*, 31 January: 3.

Brockington, D. (2000) Citizens are hard to judge, *Times Educational Supplement*, 28 April: 17.

Bryson, B. (1995) *Notes from a Small Island*. London: Black Swan.

Bunting, C. (1999) Labour hits back at 'elitist' attackers, *Times Educational Supplement*, 23 July: 6.

Campaign for Music in the Curriculum (1998) *The Fourth R: The Case for Music in the Curriculum*. Wix Hill House, Epsom Road, West Horsley, Surrey KT24 6DZ.

Cassidy, S. (2000a) Blunkett asked to sacrifice GCSEs, *Times Educational Supplement*, 14 January: 1.

Cassidy, S. (2000b) 'Maverick' takes the helm, *Times Educational Supplement*, 21 April: 3.

Cohen, N. (2000) Hit the target and miss the point, *New Statesman*, 31 January: 10.

Commons Education and Employment Select Committee (1999) *Access for All – A Survey of Post-16 Participation*. London: The Stationery Office.

Cunningham, A. (1999) Brilliance that cannot be inspected, *Times Educational Supplement*, 8 October: 21.

Davies, N. (1999) How a Tory political coup bred educational disaster, *The Guardian*, 16 September: 4.

Dean, C. (1999) Grammars 'add less value', *Times Educational Supplement*, 3 March: 3.

Dean, C. (1999) Extra 1.8bn for education, *Times Educational Supplement*, 3 December: 4.

Dean, C. (2000) How music may bring harmony, *Times Educational Supplement*, 14 January: 12.

Dean, C. and Rafferty, F. (1998) Grammar schools 'must do better', *Times Educational Supplement*, 30 October: 1.

DES (1967) *The Plowden Report: Children and Their Primary Schools*. London: HMSO.

DfEE (1997) *Excellence in Schools*. London: DfEE publications.

DfEE (1998) *Higher Education for the 21st Century: Response to the Dearing Report*. London: DfEE publications.

DfEE (1999a) *Excellence in Cities*. London: DfEE publications.

DfEE (1999b) *Sure Start*. London: DfEE publications.

DfEE (1999c) *Preparing Young People for Adult Life: A Report by the National Advisory Group on Personal, Social and Health Education*. London: DfEE Publications.

DfEE (1999d) *Bridging the Gap: New Opportunities for 16–18 Year Olds Not in Education, Employment or Training*. Report by the Social Exclusion Unit. London: DfEE Publications.

DfEE (1999e) *All our Futures: Creativity, Culture and Education*. London: DfEE publications.

DfEE (2000) *Raising Aspirations in the 21st Century*. London: DfEE publications.

Dunford, J. (2000) Blurred vision is welcome, *Times Educational Supplement*, 21 January: 19.
Estes, R. (1984) *The Social Progress of Nations*. New York: Praeger.
Gardner, H. (1983) *Frames of Mind*. New York, NY: Basic Books.
Gardner, H. (1994) The theory of multiple intelligences, in B. Moon and A. Mayes (eds) *Teaching and Learning in the Secondary School*. London: Routledge.
Handy, C. (1994) *The Empty Raincoat: Making Sense of the Future*. London: Arrow Books.
Hargreaves, D. (1994) *The Mosaic of Learning: Schools and Teachers for the Next Century*. London: Demos.
Hastrup, B. (1995) *Contemporary Danish Society: Danish Democracy and Social Welfare*. Copenhagen: Academic Press.
Higham, A. (1995) *Tomorrow's School*. Leicester: Secondary Heads Association.
Higham, A. (1998) 'Do we really need these exam boards?', *Times Educational Supplement*, 18 September: 15.
Hills, J. (1998) *Income and Wealth: The Latest Evidence*. York: Joseph Rowntree Foundation.
Hoeg, P. (1994) *Miss Smilla's Feeling for Snow*. London: Flamingo .
Hoeg, P. (1995) *Borderliners*. London: Harvill Press.
Hutton, W. (1999) 'Real cost of the property boom,' *Observer*, 15 August: 26.
Illich, I. (1971) *De-schooling Society*. London: Penguin.
Industrial Society (1997) *Speaking Up Speaking Out: The 2020 Vision Programme Research Report*. London: Industrial Society.
Kyriacou, C. (1998) *Essential Teaching Skills*. Cheltenham: Stanley Thornes.
Le Grand, J. (1999) 'How to cage the fat cats,' *New Statesman*, 20 July: 25–7.
LSE (1999) *Secondary Education Across Europe: Curricula and School Examination Systems*. London: London School of Economics.
McCarthy, C. (1999) Taxing questions on the welfare state, *Financial Times*, 17 December: 10.
Ministry of Education in Denmark (1998a) *The Education System*. Copenhagen: Undervisningsministeriet.
Ministry of Education in Denmark (1998b) *Uddannelsessystemet I tal gennem 150 ar*. Copenhagen: Undervisningsministeriet.
Moore, S. (1999) I'd rather sacrifice my children to my political beliefs than for the sake of an A level grade or two, *New Statesman*, 26 February: 17.
Morgan, C. and Morris, G. (1999) *Good Teaching and Learning: Pupils and Teachers Speak*. Buckingham: Open University Press.
Mortimore, P. (1994) Glimpse of Tomorrow, *Managing Schools Today*, November: 9–11.
National Commission on Education (1993) *Learning to Succeed*. London: Heinemann.
O'Farrell, J. (1999) *Things Can Only Get Better*. London: Black Swan.
Passmore, B. (1998) Ten years on and Ken's still pleased with himself, *Times Educational Supplement*, 23 January: 7.
Passmore, B. (1999) Bastions for the elite? *Times Educational Supplement*, 31 December: 30.
Prime Minister's Office (1999) The Government's Annual Report for 1998/99. London: HMSO.

Pring, R. (1995) *Closing the Gap: Liberal Education and Vocational Preparation*. London: Hodder and Stoughton.

Pring, R. (2000) *Philosophical Issues in Educational Research*. London: Cassell.

QCA (Qualifications and Curriculum Authority) (1998) *Education for Citizenship and the Teaching of Democracy in Schools*. Final report of the Advisory Group on Citizenship, 22 September. London: QCA.

Rafferty, F. (1999) UK puts teenagers through exam mill, *Times Educational Supplement*, 30 July: 1.

Reddy, G. (1993) *Danes are like that: perspectives of an Indian Anthropologist on the Danish Society*. Denmark: Grevas Forlag, Morke.

Reich, R. (1999) Give £50,000 to every boy and girl, *New Statesman*, 14 June: 15–16.

Rudduck, J. (ed.) (1996) *School Improvement: What Can Pupils Tell Us?* London: David Fulton Publishers.

Rudduck, J. and Maden, M. (1999) What the learners told us, *Times Educational Supplement*, 6 August: 13.

Rutter, M. *et al* (1979) *Fifteen Thousand Hours*. Wells: Open Books.

St. John-Brooks, C. (2000) Education is still my number one priority, *Times Educational Supplement*, 21 January: 4–5.

Save the Children (1999) *Our World 2000*. London: Macmillan Children's Books.

Sieghart, M. (2000) Don't let me tax anyone's credulity, *The Times*, 21 January: 24.

Slater, J. (2000) Hardest nut yet to be cracked, *Times Educational Supplement*, 31 March: 22.

Spencer, D. (1998) Sounds of civilisation, *Times Educational Supplement*, 1 May: 23.

Sutcliffe, J. (2000) 'Week in perspective,' *Times Educational Supplement*, 7 January: 18.

Tate, N. (1998) A wish list for the curriculum, *Education Review*. London: National Union of Teachers.

Tate, N. (2000) Breadth with depth, *Times Educational Supplement*, 14 January: 17.

TES editorial (1999) Farewell to GCSE?, *Times Educational Supplement*, 30 July: 10.

Thaning, K. (1982) *NFS Grundtvig*. Copenhagen: Det Danske Selskab.

Thornton, K. (1999) The Oratory and its overdraft, *Times Educational Supplement*, 1 October: 10.

Toynbee, P. (1999) A very good deal, *The Guardian*, 26 November: 7.

Vestager, M. (2000) *Vaerdier I Virkeligheden* [Values in Reality]. Copenhagen: Ministry of Education.

White, R.C. (1997) *Curriculum Innovation: A Celebration of Classroom Practice*. Buckingham: Open University Press.

White, R. (1999a) Education, *Venue*, 5 February: 85 and A question of class, *Venue*, 21 September: 14. Published by Venue, Bristol BS6 5AQ.

White, R. (1999b) Feedback, *Bristol Evening Post*, 22 December: 11.

White, R. with Brockington, D. (1983) *Tales out of School: Consumers' Views of British Education*. London: Routledge and Kegan Paul.

Wilby, P. (1998) Time to bring back Keynes: could we learn to love the taxman?, *New Statesman*, 4 September: 4–15.

Wilby, P. (2000) How to make them pay up, *New Statesman*, 24 January: 5.

Woodhead, C. (2000) Old values for the new age, *Times Educational Supplement*, 7 January: 13.

Woods, P. (1995) *Teaching*, EU208 in Exploring Educational Issues, Unit 2. Milton Keynes: The Open University.

Wragg, E. (2000) 'Graves we should dance on,' *Times Educational Supplement*, 7 January: 28.

Young, S. (1993) Curriculum risks lives, *Times Educational Supplement*, 26 March: 3.

# Index

# IMAGES OF EDUCATIONAL CHANGE

## Herbert Altrichter and John Elliott

This important book takes a fresh look at educational change – a concept which is in frequent use but rarely examined for the variety of meanings it conveys. It brings together the ideas of major educational change theorists from three continents, and invites the reader to explore the idea of educational change at a number of levels and from a variety of perspectives.

There is much talk about the pace of social change in, and the growing complexity of, industrial societies. In this book a number of well-known international researchers attempt to analyse the meaning of contemporary social change for education.

Particular emphasis is given to the implications for:

- the personal and social development of students
- schools as organizations
- the school curriculum
- the teaching profession
- educational policy formation
- education research.

*Contents*
*Introduction – Part 1: Educational change and policy formation – Part 2: The relationship between social and educational change – Part 3: Conceptualizing school change processes – Part 4: Preparing teachers for creative engagement with educational change – Overview – Towards a synoptic vision of educational change in advanced industrial societies – Index.*

240pp    0 335 20188 1 (Paperback)    0 335 20189 X (Hardback)

# LEADING SCHOOLS IN TIMES OF CHANGE

Christopher Day, Alma Harris, Mark Hadfield, Harry Tolley and John Beresford

> ... a refreshing and rigorous, evidence-based view of the challenges, joys and headaches of being a successful headteacher ...
>
> Mick Brookes, President, National Association of Headteachers

> ... a significant contribution to our understanding of the qualities those in, and aspiring to, school leader roles need to possess and to further develop.
>
> Kenneth Leithwood, Centre for Leadership Development,
> OISE, University of Toronto

> ... a superbly balanced book at the cutting edge of writing on school leadership.
>
> Brian Caldwell, Dean of Education, University of Melbourne

> A must read for anyone serious about improving schools.
>
> Thomas J. Sergiovanni, Lillian Radford Professor of Education
> and Administration at Trinity University, USA

Leadership of schools in changing times is fraught with opportunities and challenges. This book considers effective leadership and management of schools from the perspectives of headteachers, teachers, students, ancillaries, governors and parents in a variety of reputationally good schools of different phases, locations and sizes. Through a mixture of participants' accounts and analysis of leadership theory, this highly readable book reveals a number of characteristics of headteachers who are both effective and successful: the centrality of personal values, people-centred leadership and the ability to manage tensions and dilemmas. The authors propose a post-transformational theory that reflects the complexity of leadership behaviour in the twenty-first century, suggesting that reliance upon rational, managerialist theory as the basis for training is inappropriate for the values-led contingency model that is necessary to lead schools successfully in times of change.

## Contents

224pp    0 335 20582 8 (Paperback)    0 335 20583 6 (Hardback)